First published in Great Britain in 2009 by Prion Books
an imprint of the Carlton Publishing Group
20 Mortimer Street
London W1T 3JW

A catalogue record for this book is available from the British Library.

ISBN 978-1-85375-739-6

10 9 8 7 6 5 4 3 2 1

Printed in the UK by CPI Mackays, Chatham, ME5 8TD

The content of this book was previously published as
The Zoo Rude Jokes Book in 2005 and *The Zoo Book of Laughs* in 2007.

ZOO's BIGGEST BOOK OF LAUGHS EVER!

A bulging book full of the funniest
stuff from your favourite men's mag!

PRION

CONTENTS

SPORT:
QUOTES & JOKES

"You know, I always thought football was a bit gay."

Sly Stallone, who oddly wasn't brave enough to
say it during a trip to Goodison Park

"Why would I want to give every penny I've earned to some horrible little chav footballer so he can buy his wife dresses to wear at Aintree? I'd rather piss it up the wall."

Noel Gallagher rules himself out of buying Manchester City

"In my past 10 games I've scored 10 goals. Could I be any better?"

No, it's not Cristiano Ronaldo. It's Marek Saganowski. Of Southampton

"Ninety minutes before a game there is not much a coach can do. You can't talk to players, so you sit drinking tea."

Former England boss Sven-Goran Eriksson
neatly sums up his five-year reign

"He's tall/He's mad/He dances like your dad/Peter Crouch/ Peter Crouch"

Favoured chant from England fans

"I did not have any nerves, although I did go to the toilet just before I came on so there might have been some there."

Theo Walcott reveals his Arsenal debut preparations

"We need to score from midfield. I told the players 'Frankie Lampard's got 17'. They just said 'Perhaps that's why he's on 150-odd grand a week'."

Harry Redknapp, in his Portsmouth days, 50 gets a reality check

"Rooney was protesting and complaining all the time. Wah wah wah. He reminded me of my kids."

Horacio Elizondo, the referee who sent off Wazza in the 2006 World Cup England vs Porrtugal quarter-final

"I watch a lot more football these days than when I was younger. I never really went to games then, as I was playing."

Shaun Wright-Philips looks on the bright side of life on the substitutes bench

"We were able to test ourselves against better players. And the showers were warm – we're not used to that."

Yeading FC skipper Nevin Saroya speaking after losing 5–0 to Nottingham Forest in the FA Cup

"Wayne Rooney is like me, both as a player and a person. He comes from a rough area and I like that."

Diego Maradona sees a little of himself in England's golden boy

"Are you shagging Elton John?"

Newcastle fans to the Watford end

"Are you shagging Ant 'n' Dec?"

The Watford supporters respond

"Football is football and everyone sniffs around everyone else's back door."

Stuart Pearce lets slip on activities in the shower room

"This is absolutely fantastic – it's better than sex!"

Jockey Robbie Power after winning the Grand National on Silver Birch

"You might get some now, then!"

Trainer Gordon Elliott's instant reply

"I broke the legs of four players and a couple of arms… And that was just our team in training."

No wonder Brit boxer David "Hayemaker" Haye was banned from school football

"I used to milk 100 cows, six days a week, and then go out to a place like Newbridge in Wales on a wet Wednesday night and have my head kicked in. And do you know what? I miss those days."

England rugby union player Phil Vickery looks back on his time as a farmer and amateur player

"They remind me a bit of Laurel and Hardy… er… in that they are different characters who complement each other nicely."

Shane Warne on Flintoff and Strauss

"Stan Collymore once got beaten up by big rugby players. They say Stan was bragging about having a fight with a rugby player outside a pub and giving him a good hiding. But he didn't say that at all. What he actually said was the last time he was in a car park, he splattered an Austin Healey."

Frank Skinner

It's the final game of the 2003/4 season. Martin Keown needs just one more appearance to collect his Premiership winner's medal. With one minute to go, Wenger signals for his third and final substitution. Keown and Ray Parlour are both warming up. "Ray," shouts assistant manager Pat Rice, "get stripped off." With his last chance of silverwear disappearing over the horizon, Keown goes ballistic – only to realise that the whole Arsenal bench is laughing and pointing at him. He was going to be brought on all the time! What jolly japes!

The old 'Is That A Lump Of Shit In Your Hand Or Are You Just Pleased To See Me' trick, as described by Razor Ruddock:

"Steve Sedgley came up and shook my hand to wish me well before a match. It wasn't until I'd run on the pitch that I realised my hand was caked in shit. It stunk and I had to spend the rest of the half trying to get it off."

This from a man who used to piss his pants to warm himself up on a cold day.

"I'd say about 50% of the squads I'm in these days shave their legs and use fake tan."

Gavin Henson endears himself even more to team-mates

The England and New Zealand rugby coaches both die and enter the Pearly Gates. God takes the England coach on a tour of heaven and ends up at a little two-bedroom bungalow with a faded English rugby banner hanging from the front porch. "This is your house," says God, "You're very lucky. Most people don't get their own houses up here, you know." He looks at the house, nods, and then turns around and notices a huge mansion on top of the hill with All-Black banners lining both sides of the footpath and a huge New Zealand flag hanging between the massive marble columns. "Thanks for the house, God," he says, "but how come I get this little bungalow when he gets a huge mansion?" God looks at him seriously for a moment. "What do you mean?" He says. "That's my house."

When Faustino Asprilla arrived in Newcastle, he was desperate to find out what was 'hip' and 'trendy' in the UK at the time. So the squad marched the Colombian striker straight down to Newcastle's hottest clothing emporium – the local Disney store – and kitted him out with a natty Daffy Duck waistcoat and tie combo. Tino could never understand the funny looks he got when he was 'out' on the 'toon'.

"If I'm looking good, it'll give me that extra edge. It's all part of the routine – shaving my legs, putting on fake tan and doing my hair."

Gavin Henson's camp pre-match grooming ritual

"According to recent Government figures, in the last three years 600,000 immigrants have come to England to seek work – half of them in the Premiership."

Dara Ó Briain – Mock The Week

"I have to answer the phone a lot more and I'm no good at that. I have a face for radio without the voice. I've also got to find a matchday suit that fits me."

Sammy Lee ponders his job

"Wayne Rooney is a bull, so strong he'd be perfect for any job. Including helping you move house."

Spain's Michel Salgado pays tribute

"My God, it's like 'do you want to die or do you want to die?'"

Thierry Henry is asked to choose between never scoring again or never having sex again

"I had a dream about Didier Drogba the other night. He's gorgeous. I came into work all distressed because it had gone wrong at the end."

GMTV's Fiona Phillips likes a big striker up top

"I just sit in my brothel alone watching TV. Men are not interested they're wet and beer-sodden. It's a catastrophe."

German prostitute on how the 2006 World Cup has been bad for business

"I've prepared some new tricks, like something out of *The Matrix*."

Cristiano Ronaldo bends over backwards for his country

"Players should masturbate consistently. It doesn't wear them out, is a major physical boost and stops them chasing skirt."

Leading sexologist Germanico Zambrano advising Ecuador's national team

"I can understand that people say I'm arrogant. I saw myself walking on the TV not so long ago and I thought to myself 'That's an unpleasant posture – can't I change the way I walk?'"

Arsenal's Robin van Persie does some soul-searching

"I praise my son for defending the family's honour and have nothing but contempt for Materazzi. I want his balls on a platter."

The furious mother of Zinedine Zidane after his 2006 World Cup shame

"Maybe Big Sam's pushed Anelka's bed up against the wall so he can only get out on the good side."

Paul Merson on Nicolas Anelka's consistent form for Bolton

"It's like Amsterdam. They look great in the window, but turn out to be dogs."

Comic Bob Mills on the perils of the transfer window

"What a complete chicken nugget with double barbecue sauce he is."

Ex-Plymouth boss Ian Holloway after Paul Connolly is injured

"I got bombed. I made sure I was in the same team as the lads who aren't being picked, but I still think they were shooting at me."

Roy Keane on Sunderland's team-bonding paintball session

"Noel drags it out a little bit, but *Deal or No Deal* is still pretty good. I switch off once the big money boxes have gone, though."

So that's how Michael Owen's spends his time when he's injured

"Ryan could play football in a phone box and find the door, no matter how many players you put in there with him."

Man Utd assistant coach Carlos Queiroz's tribute to Ryan Giggs. Er... right

"Cristiano Ronaldo goes down too easy for my liking but remember, he's literally had two big men up his backside for 90 minutes."

Tony Gale hits innuendo overload on Sky Sports

"I feel very determined and really hungry."

Once-fat footballer Frank Lampard's comments about his focus on the pitch get misconstrued

"What the national coaches are doing is like taking a car from your garage without asking permission. They then use the car for ten days and abandon it in a field without any petrol left in the tank. We then have to recover it, but it is broken down."

Arsenal boss Arsene Wenger, whose 1st XI comprises international players, knows the feeling

"We passed like ships in the night. He was a huge rich yacht and I was a little rowing boat."

Graeme le Saux on leaving Chelsea just as Roman Abramovich arrived

"People are entitled to their opinion. Not that I'll ever watch *Without A Trace* again."

Former Sydney FC Coach Terry Butcher on actor and shareholder Anthony LaPaglia's call for his head

"Sir David Beckham? You're having a laugh. He's just a good footballer with a famous bird."

Blackpool manager Ian Holloway isn't impressed by talk of a knighthood for David Beckham

"If you're a superstar and earn more than anybody else, you have to lead from the front. They didn't. At times they behaved like shits."

Danish International Thomas Gravesen talks frankly about his time at Real Madrid

"If it was a boxing match, it'd be Muhammad Ali against Jimmy Krankie."

Aidy Boothroyd on Watford taking on Man United

"It didn't take that robotic dance to make Peter Crouch look freaky – he already looks like a terminally ill child crossed with a flamingo."

Frankie Boyle

After a disastrous match, former England boss Sven Goran Eriksson yells:'Heskey, you were crap.'

David Beckham tries to reassure his team-mate: 'Don't listen to him, Emile. He doesn't know what he's talking about. He just repeats what everybody else says.'

An Aberdeen fan is trapped on a desert island, alone apart from a sheep and a dog.

Soon, the sheep begins to look very attractive to the Aberdeen fan.

The problem is, however, that whenever he approaches the sheep, the dog growls threateningly.

The Aberdeen fan takes the dog to the opposite side of the island, giving it some food as a distraction. He runs back to the sheep, only to find the dog has made it back first, and is still growling at him.

Next, the Aberdeen fan ties the dog to a tree with a long leash. He goes back to the sheep, only to find the dog still growling, this time with a gnawed-off leash round its neck.

The Aberdeen fan begins to get more and more sexually frustrated. Then, as he sits under a palm tree staring out to sea, a beautiful young woman in a sexy bikini emerges from the surf.

She asks him who he is and, taking pity on him, asks if there's anything she can do tonight to stop him feeling lonely.

The Aberdeen fan thinks for a moment and says: 'Could you take the dog for a walk?'

Q. What should you do if a Birmingham fan throws a grenade at you?

A. Pull the pin out and throw it back.

Q. Why do Arsenal fans smell?
A. So the blind can hate them as well.

Q. Why do Chelsea fans whistle while they're sitting on the toilet?
A. So they know which end to wipe.

A Celtic-supporting van driver used to keep himself amused by scaring every Rangers fan he saw sauntering down the street.

He would swerve as if to hit them, and at the last minute, swerve back on to the road.

One day, as he was driving, he saw a priest hitch-hiking. He thought he would do his good deed for the day and offer the priest a lift.

The driver says, 'Where are you off to, Father?'

The priest says, 'I'm going to give Mass at St Michael's Church. It's about two miles down the road.'

The driver says, 'No problem. Jump in.'

The priest climbs aboard and they set off.

Suddenly the driver sees a Rangers fan walking along the pavement, and instinctively swerves as if to hit him. But just in time he remembers that there's a priest in his van, so swerves back on to the road again, narrowly missing the Rangers fan.

But although he's sure he didn't hit him, he still hears a loud thud.

Wondering where the noise came from, he glances in his mirrors and, seeing nothing, says to the priest, 'I'm worried, Father. I just missed that Rangers fan who was walking down the road.'

The priest says, 'No need to worry. I got the bastard with the door.'

A man distraught about Charlton's poor form prepares to hang himself.

He decides to wear his full Charlton Athletic kit.

A neighbour discovers the body and tells a policeman.

On arrival, the policeman quickly removes the dead man's Charlton kit and dresses him in stockings and suspenders.

Baffled, the neighbour asks why.

The policeman says, 'It's to avoid embarrassing the family.'

An Evertonian undertaker takes on an apprentice.

The apprentice walks up to his first corpse and examines it. He rolls it over and is amazed to find a cork stuck in the corpse's arsehole.

Mystified, he pulls it out and hears the strains of 'You'll Never Walk Alone' coming out.

Startled, he quickly shoves the cork back in and runs off to find his boss.

He says, 'You've got to come and help me. I've just found a cork in one of the corpse's arseholes, and you won't believe what happens when you pull it out!'

The old undertaker follows his assistant, and is mildly surprised to see that there is indeed a cork plugging the body's back door.

He pulls it out, and again, the strains of 'You'll Never Walk Alone' can be heard emanating from the orifice.

The undertaker turns to his assistant and says, 'What's so surprising? You can hear 40,000 arseholes singing that every other Saturday.'

A teacher asks all the children what their dads do for a living.

All the usual answers come up: salesman, builder, fireman and so on.

But little Johnny doesn't raise his hand.

The teacher says, 'Come on, Johnny. We want to know what your dad does.'

Johnny says, 'My dad is an exotic dancer in a gay club and takes off all his clothes in front of other men. Sometimes, if the offer's really good, he goes out with a man, rents a cheap hotel room and lets them sleep with him.'

The teacher quickly sets the other children some work and takes little Johnny aside to ask him if that was really true.

Johnny says, 'No, he plays football for Scotland, but I was too embarrassed to say.'

Q. What's the difference between a dead dog in the road and a dead Manchester United fan in the road?
A. The dog has skid marks in front of it.

Two Everton fans are in a pub.

The first one says, 'You know something? I was so pissed off with the team the other day that I nailed my season ticket to the club gates.'

The second one says, 'But that's money down the drain, isn't it?'

The first one says, 'That's what I thought. So the next day I went back for it – only to find that some bastard had nicked my nail.'

An old man and his wife are in bed.

After lying there for a few minutes, the old man farts and shouts, 'Goal!'

His wife says, 'What the hell was that?'

The old man says, 'I'm ahead one-nil.'

A few minutes later, the wife lets one go and shouts, 'Goal! One-all!'

After another ten minutes, the old man farts again. 'Goal! Two-one!'

The wife quickly farts again and shouts, 'Goal! Two-all!'

Not to be outdone, the old man strains as hard as he can to squeeze out the winning fart.

Unfortunately, he tries too hard and shits the bed.

His wife says, 'What the hell was that?'

The old man says, 'Half-time. Swap sides…'

David James is so despondent after his latest blunder he decides to end it all, so he throws himself down in front of a number 57 bus. Luckily, it passes under him.

A nurse is walking through the hospital when she sees two doctors fighting.

She breaks them up and yells, 'Why are you fighting?'

The first doctor says, 'It's that guy on E Ward – the one with the Man United pyjamas. Dr Jones here has just told him that he's only got two weeks left to live.'

The nurse says, 'But here was really nothing more we could do for the man – he just had to be told.'

The first doctor says, 'I know that, but I wanted to be the one who got to tell the bastard.'

Four surgeons are taking a tea break.

The first surgeon says, 'Accountants are the best to operate on, because when you open them up, everything inside is numbered.'

The second surgeon says, 'No, librarians are the best. Everything inside them is in alphabetical order.'

The third surgeon says, 'You should try electricians. Everything inside them is colour-coded.'

The fourth surgeon says, 'I prefer Tottenham fans. They're heartless, spineless, gutless and their heads and arses are interchangeable.'

A woman visits her doctor and tells him, 'I keep hearing the sound of "Glory, Glory Man United" coming from my crotch!'

'Don't worry about it,' the doctor says, 'a lot of twats sing that.'

Q. What's the difference between a Millwall fan and an onion?
A. No one would cry if you chopped up a Millwall fan.

Q. What's the difference between a porcupine and the Newcastle team bus?
A. The porcupine has pricks on the outside.

Q. How many Manchester United fans does it take to pave a driveway?
A. Depends how thin you slice them.

Liverpool sign a player from Kosovo.

On his debut he scores a hat-trick as Liverpool come from two down to win.

After the game, he calls home and tells his mother what an amazing day he's had.

She says, 'I'm so pleased for you, but things aren't so great over here. Today, dad's been shot, I got beaten and robbed and your sister's been raped.'

The player says, 'That's terrible, mum. But you understand that it was for the good of all of us that I left home and came to Liverpool, don't you?'

His mum says, 'Of course, but did you have to bring us with you?'

Q. What do you call 20 Leeds fans sky-diving?

A. Diarrhoea.

Q. What's the difference between a Manchester United fan and a vibrator?

A. A Manchester United fan is a real dick.

Q. What do you call a Norwich City fan with a girlfriend?

A. A shepherd.

Sophie Ellis Bextor has been found headbutted to death in the apartment of a French footballer.

Apparently it was murder on Zidane's floor.

A teacher starts a new job at a school on Merseyside and, trying to make a good impression on her first day, explains to her class that she is a Liverpool fan.

She asks her students to raise their hands if they, too, are Liverpool fans.

Everyone in the class raises their hand except one little girl.

The teacher looks at her and says, 'Mary, why didn't you raise your hand?'

Mary says, 'Because I'm not a Liverpool fan.'

The teacher says, 'If you're not a Liverpool fan, who are you a fan of?'

Mary says, 'I'm a Manchester United fan.'

The teacher says, 'Why?'

Mary says, 'Because my mum is a United fan and my dad is a United fan, so I'm a United fan, too.'

The teacher says, 'That's no reason for you to be a United fan. You don't have to be just like your parents all the time. What if your mum was a prostitute and your dad was a drug addict – what would you be then?'

Mary says, 'A Liverpool fan.'

Q. What do United fans use as birth control?
A. Their personalities.

David Beckham has turned down a move to Newcastle United.

Real Madrid and Newcastle had agreed a £15 million transfer fee for the England star.

But Beckham said there was no way he could join Newcastle after what the Toon Army had done to Thailand.

A Manchester United fan dies on match day and goes to heaven wearing his Manchester United shirt.

He knocks on the pearly gates and out walks St Peter.

St Peter says, 'Sorry, no Manchester United fans allowed in Heaven.'

Astounded, the Manchester United fan says, 'But I've been a good man!'

St Peter says, 'Oh, really? What have you done?'

The Manchester United fan says, 'Three weeks before I died, I gave £10 to **Save the Children**.'

St Peter says, 'Hmm... Anything else?'

The Manchester United fan says, 'Two weeks before I died, I gave £10 to the homeless.'

St Peter says, 'Hmm... Anything else?'

The Manchester United fan says, 'A week before I died, I gave £10 to the Albanian orphans.'

'Very well,' St Peter says, 'Wait here a minute while I have a word with the boss.'

Two minutes later, St Peter returns.

'I've had a word with God,' he says, 'and he agrees with me. Here's your £30 back; now fuck off.'

The Post Office has recalled its new set of Manchester United-themed stamps.

People couldn't work out which side to spit on.

Before a friendly between England and Scotland, Wayne Rooney walks into the dressing room to discover that half the team is asleep.

Rooney says, 'What's going on?'

David Beckham says, 'We just can't motivate ourselves, because it's only Scotland.'

Rooney says, 'Tell you what, lads, why don't you have a rest down the pub, and I'll face them myself?'

So the team goes to the pub.

After a while, they wonder how the match is going and get the landlord to put the match on TV.

The scoreline at the top of the screen says, 'England 1 Scotland 0: Wayne Rooney, 10 minutes.' The players cheer, then turn the telly off and return to their drinks.

After a while, Rio Ferdinand says, 'It'll be full time now. Let's see how Wayne got on.'

The final score comes up as, 'England 1 Scotland 1: Barry Ferguson, 89 minutes.'

The England players rush to the stadium to congratulate Rooney.

However, they find him crying.

Rooney says, 'I'm really sorry, lads – I let you down.'

Beckham says, 'Don't be daft. You drew with Scotland all on your own!'

Rooney says, 'But I'm so ashamed: I got sent off in the 12th minute.'

Q. How do you kill a Palace fan while he's drinking?
A. Slam the toilet seat on his head.

Rio Ferdinand goes to the doctor.

The doctor says, 'I've got some bad news and some good news for you.'

Rio says, 'What is it?'

The doctor says, 'The bad news is your grandmother has died.'

Distraught, the footballer says, 'Oh my God, no! So what's the good news?'

The doctor says, 'Well at least Wayne Rooney can't shag her now.'

A woman goes to her doctor and says, 'Can you get pregnant from anal sex?'

The doctor says, 'Of course. Where do you think Leicester fans come from?'

Wayne Rooney goes to the doctor and says, 'I don't understand it. Every time I look in the mirror, I become sexually excited.'

The doctor says, 'That's because you look like a twat.'

Q. How does Wayne Rooney hit two balls at the same time?

A. By stepping on a rake.

Sven Goran Eriksson spots a turd on England's training pitch.

He shouts, 'Who's shit on the ground?'

Emile Heskey says, 'I am, boss, but I'm OK in the air.'

Steve Waugh? I reckon he'd sledge his own kids in a game of backyard cricket. He'd say: "I had sex with your mother last night!"

Will Anderson

The seven dwarves are in a cave when suddenly it collapses.

Snow White is frightened for their lives, until she hears a voice from inside the cave saying, 'Tottenham are good enough to qualify for the Champions League.'

She says, 'Thank Christ; at least Dopey's all right.'

Three football fans are walking home when they see a naked woman lying dead in the middle of the street.

After they call the police, they each take off their hats and place them on the dead woman to cover her up until the cops arrive. The first fan places his Spurs hat over her left breast, the second places his Chelsea hat over her right breast, and the third fan places his Arsenal hat over her crotch.

The policeman arrives and examines the body.

He lifts the Spurs hat and quickly replaces it. Then he lifts the Chelsea cap and quickly replaces it.

However, when he lifts the Arsenal hat, he stares for what feels like ages.

Finally, he lets the hat drop and turns to walk away.

The fans are curious, and ask him why he spent so much time inspecting the woman's vagina.

The policeman says, 'It's the first time I've seen anything other than an arsehole under an Arsenal hat.'

Q. Which are the three English teams with swear words in their name?

A. Arse-nal, S-cunt-horpe and Manchester fucking United.

Q. What's three feet long and keeps a twat warm?

A. A Manchester United scarf.

Q. What do Newcastle fans and laxatives have in common?

A. Both irritate the crap out of you.

You're trapped in a room with a tiger, a rattlesnake and an Arsenal fan. You have a gun with two bullets. What should you do?

Shoot the Arsenal fan twice.

Q. What whistles and licks Sir Alex Ferguson's arse?

A. A Premiership referee.

What have Wormwood Scrubs and Old Trafford at 4.45pm got in common?

They're both full of Cockneys trying to get out.

Q. How many Manchester United fans does it take to change a lightbulb?

A. Three. One to change the bulb, one to buy the "2005 Lightbulb Changing" commemorative DVD, one to drive the other two back to Torquay.

"A new survey says over half of sick days are claimed falsely, and many of these fake sickies coincide with sporting events. For example, a lot of people failed to turn up during the Cricket World Cup. Half the England team, for example."

Steve Punt, The Now Show

Michael Owen walks into a nightclub, goes straight up to a girl, starts feeling her tits and says, 'Get your coat, sexy, you're coming home with me.'
  The girl says, 'You're a little forward.'

Manchester United Viruses:
  • The Manchester United Fan Virus – your computer develops a memory disorder and forgets about everything before 1993.
  • The Manchester United Shirt Virus – This one is especially hard to detect as it changes format every three months.
  • The Ronaldo Virus – The computer looks great, all the lights are on, but nothing inside works.
  • The Roy Keane Virus – Kicks you out of Windows.
  • The Alex Ferguson Virus – The computer develops a continuous whining noise. The on screen clock runs slower than all the other computers in the building.
  • The Tim Howard Virus – The computer looks like it's functioning normally but you can't save anything.

"Britain was battered by torrential storms this week; hundreds of people have fled Wolverhampton. It wasn't raining but they found an old bus and saw an opportunity for a better life. Meanwhile, Tim Henman is thinking about getting into coaching… he's offering discount fares to all of Britain's market towns."

Jimmy Carr, 8 Out Of 10 Cats

Duncan Ferguson walks into a pub. The landlord says, "A pint of your usual, Dunc?"

Big Dunc replies, "No, just a half, then I'm off."

St James' Park was broken into last night and the entire contents of the trophy room were stolen. Newcastle police are believed to be looking for a man with a black and white carpet.

"Why did the Gers fan *never* cross the road? He was waiting for the Green Man to turn Orange."

Dylan Moran

A Geordie arrives in hell and is welcomed by the Devil. "So, how do you find this place?" asks Satan.

"Why aye man, it's a canny place you've got here," replies the Mag.

The Devil's a bit miffed so cranks up the thermostat. The next day, he seeks out the Geordie and asks, "So, how do you like it now?"

"It's top, man," he replies. "Reminds me of me summer hols to Spain."

So the heat gets cranked up as high as it'll go. Again the Devil finds the Geordie, and again the Geordie remarks on how pleasant it is. By now, Satan's absolutely furious, and turns the thermometer all the way down. The next morning, Satan tracks down the Geordie and demands, "OK, smart-arse, how do you like it *now*?"

With icicles hanging from every part of his body, the Geordie just about shivers out, "Eh, pet, does this mean wor team's won the cup?"

"I was shocked by David Pleat's slanderous comments about the Man United Wags during this week's win. Especially his accusation that 'Smith's chance was even easier than Saha's missus.'"

Off The Fiver

Nigel Worthington is queuing in his local building society when a gunman bursts in through the door demanding money. Nige attempts to tackle the raider, but the gunman twats him on the head and knocks him out cold. The robber escapes and the cashier tries to revive the Norwich City manager. After a few minutes he comes round looking bewildered. His first words are "Where the hell am I?"

The cashier replies: "Don't worry, Mr Worthington, sir. You're in the Nationwide."

"Fuck me," replies Nigel, "Is it August already?"

"Me and about eight mates went up Chelsea last week. Bill Clinton was fucking furious."

Frank Skinner

Q. What does Cheryl Tweedy get when she offers Ashley Cole a penny for his thoughts?
A. Change.

Two Irishmen are fishing. The first reels in his line and sees that he's snagged an old bottle. As he's taking it off the hook, a genie pops out and promises to grant him one wish.

"Turn the lake into beer," he says. The genie goes "Poof!" and the lake turns into beer.

Second Irishman says, "You jerk. Now we've got to piss in the boat."

What do you call a Chelsea fan on the moon?
A Problem.
What do you call 100 Chelsea fans on the moon?
An even bigger problem.
What do you call *all* the Chelsea fans on the moon?
Problem solved.

Why is the Portsmouth football team like a possum?
Because they play dead at home and they get killed on the road.

Two blokes are walking through a cemetery when they happen upon a tombstone that reads: 'Here lies John Sweeney, a good man and a Chelsea fan.' One of the men turns to the other and asks, "When the hell did they start putting two people in one grave?"

What's the difference Keiron Dyer and a computer?
You only have to punch information into a computer once.

Why does Alan Shearer drink his tea from a bowl?
Because he's lost all his cups.

Man City have a new line of cologne. It's a little different though; you wear it and the other guy scores.

What's the difference between OJ Simpson and Newcastle?
OJ had a more credible defence.

What would you get if Man U were relegated?
45,000 more Chelsea fans.

The fire brigade phones Harry Redknapp in the early hours of Sunday morning.
"Mr Redknapp sir, White Hart Lane is on fire!"
"The cups man! Save the cups!" replies Redknapp.
"No need to worry – the fire hasn't spread to the canteen yet, sir."

"Sport: essentially just enormous fat people sat down, stuffing their faces, roaring their disapproval at the most finely-tuned athletes in the world."

Dylan Moran

What's the difference between a Gillingham fan and a coconut?
One's thick and hairy, the other's a tropical nut.

You see a Liverpool fan on a bike – why shouldn't you swerve to hit him?

It might be your bike.

In a small town in Northern Ireland, the local Catholic team were about to take the field against the local Protestants. "Remember, lads," said the coach, "if you can't kick the ball, kick the player's shins, and if you can't kick his shins, trip him and kick his head. Now, as soon as we find the ball we'll kick off."

"Fuck the ball," said a voice from the back. "Let's get on with the game."

What do David Beckham and trains have in common?
They both go in and out of Victoria.

What do you get if you cross the English cricket team with an Oxo cube?

A laughing stock.

"At Wimbledon, Henman has 'Henman Hill' named after him and Murray has 'Murray Mound'. Greg [Rusedski] has a bakers opposite the station."

Jimmy Carr, 8 Out Of 10 Cats

In the Norwich City dressing room…

Nigel Worthington: "Twenty teams in the League and you lot are bottom."

Darren Huckerby: "Well it could have been worse."

Nigel Worthington: "Oh really, how?"

Huckerby: "Well, there could have been more teams in the League."

Why do Arsenal players call Wenger 'Hitler'?
Because he couldn't win in Europe either.

David Beckham walks into a sperm donor bank:

"I'd like to donate some sperm," he says to the receptionist.

"Certainly sir," replies the receptionist. "Have you donated sperm before?"

"Yes," replies Beckham, "you should have my details on your computer."

"Oh yes, I've just found your details," says the receptionist, "but I see you're going to need some help. Shall I call Posh for you?"

"Why do I need help?" asks Beckham.

"Well David," the receptionist replies, "it says on your record you're a useless wanker."

Mark Hughes and Alex Ferguson are being interviewed at the end of the season, and the interviewer turns to Hughes and asks, "So Mark after a tough season, how do you see Rovers going next year?"

"Well, our main aim is just to stay in the Premier league. I think we're in with a reasonable chance."

The interviewer turns to Ferguson: "So then Alex, what do you think of United's prospects then?"

"Well I'm hoping that we'll win the Premiership, the Champions League and the FA cup and win every single game we play all season – and probably for the next ten years."

The interviewer is shocked and gasps at Ferguson, "You're not serious, surely?"

Ferguson replies, "Well Sparky started it!!"

What's the difference Jose Mourinho and God?
God doesn't think he's Jose Mourinho.

A guy comes home from golfing, and his wife asks him how it went.

"Well, we were doing fine until Bob had a heart attack and died on the fourth hole…"

"Oh my god, that's terrible!"

"You're telling me. For the rest of the afternoon, it was swing, drag Bob, swing, drag Bob…"

Patrick, a Manchester United fan, is appearing on *Who Wants To Be A Millionaire*. He's faced with the £125,000 question.

"On the screen is a photograph of a former Manchester United player as a small baby," says Tarrant. "The question is – which player is it?"

"I think it's David Beckham," says Pat, "but I'll phone my friend Mick just to make sure."

They phone Mick, another United supporter, but he's not so sure. "I think it's Peter Schmeichal," he says.

"Are you sure now Mick," says Pat, "Because I'm convinced it's David Beckham."

"Definitely," replies Mick.

Pat gives Chris his answer, and after the usual faffing about, finally says, "Sorry Pat, Peter Schmeichel is the wrong answer."

"Oh well," says Pat, "but would you mind telling me who it was, then?"

"No problem Pat," says Chris, "it was Andy Cole."

Why can't you get a cup of tea at Highbury?
All the mugs are on the field and all the cups are Stamford Bridge.

How many Man United fans does it take to change a light bulb?

540,002. That's one to change it, 40,000 to say they've been changing it for years, 500,000 to buy the replica kit, and one to compare the light bulb to George Best.

The Sultan of Brunei wanted to give his three favourite sons a Christmas present, so he asked each one what he wanted. The first said he wanted a car, so he gave him Rolls Royce Motors.

The second said he'd like a plane, so he gave him British Aerospace.

The third, and youngest, said he'd like a Mickey Mouse outfit, so he gave him Middlesbrough.

They say that hooliganism and racism are bad, but personally, we think Iain Dowie is the unacceptable face of British football.

What's the difference between Coventry and the Bermuda triangle? The Bermuda triangle has three points.

There's a rumour that after the current sponsorship expires, Forest have lined up a new sponsor – Tampax. The board thought it was appropriate as the club is going through a very bad period.

Sir Alex Ferguson goes to visit a Chelsea training session. Eventually he says to Mourinho, "Come on, what's your secret?"

Mourinho replies, "I keep my players mentally fit as well as physically fit by setting them intelligence tests." So, to demonstrate, he calls Didier Drogba over. "Didier," he says. "I am your father's son but I am not your brother. Who am I?" Drogba thinks for a few seconds and says, "Easy boss, you're Didier Drogba."

Enlightened, Fergie drives back to old Trafford and calls Ronaldo into his office. "Cristiano," he says. "I am your father's son, but I am not your brother. Who am I?" Ronaldo simply looks perplexed, so Fergie says, "OK, I'll give you a day to think about it – come back to my office with your answer tomorrow."

So Ronaldo disappears and, still confused, asks Roy Keane for help. "Keano," he says. "I am your father's son, but I am not your brother. Who am I?"

"You're me, Roy Keane," replies Keane. A look of enlightenment spreads across Ronaldo's face.

The next day Ronaldo bursts into Ferguson's office: "Boss! Boss! I've got it – you're Roy Keane!"

"Jesus Christ!" fumes Fergie. "Are you really that stupid? I'm Didier Drogba!"

What's the difference between Alan Shearer and a Mini?
A Mini can only carry three passengers.

How can you tell when Leeds are losing?
The clock says five past three.

Here's a top tip for all Manchester United fans. You don't need to waste a ton of money on expensive new kits every season. You simply strap a large inflatable penis to your forehead, and everyone will immediately know which team you support.

A Man United fan, about 8 years old, goes into sports shop to buy a United football. It's £25 but the boy only has £5, so he says to the shopkeeper, "Blindfold me and pick any football off that shelf and I bet I can guess what football team is on the ball. If I get it right you have to give me the United ball."

So he blindfolds the boy, gets the ball off the shelf and puts it in front of the boy's face. The boy shouts, "It's Wolves! – I can hear the sound of a pack of wolves in the woods." So the shopkeeper gets a ball from the shelf puts it in front of the boy's face. The boy shouts, "I'ts Arsenal! I can hear the guns on a bloody war field."

The shocked shopkeeper says, "Right, get this one and you can have the ball and the Beckham boots." So he gets the ball puts it in front of the boy's face. The boy shouts "It's Palace."

"How did you get that one?" says the shopkeeper.

The boy says, "Well, it's going down."

How many Manchester City fans does it take to change a light bulb?
None – they're quite happy living in the shadows.

A Liverpool fan sees a poster in a video shop window saying "Anfield – The Golden Years". He enters the shop and asks how much the video costs. The shop owner replies, "It's £300'". The Liverpool fan replies, "Eh? I'm not paying £300 just for a video." The shop owner replies, "Don't be soft. The video is £5, the Beta-Max player is £295."

What do Daniel Bedingfield and David Beckham have in common?

They're both fucking useless singers.

Legendary Brazilian striker Ronaldo goes into a *Burger King* and says "Give me two whoppers".

The cashier says: "Ok, You're not fat and you haven't lost it."

Q. How many Fulham supporters does it take to unscrew a lightbulb? A. Both of them.

Thierry Henry, Ronaldinho and Beckham are at the pearly gates of heaven. St Peter opens the gate, turns to Henry and asks "Why do you deserve eternal happiness in Heaven my son?"

Thierry replies: "I am an artist; I inspire young people to be great footballers, and in turn take them away from a life of crime." St Peter nods, impressed.

He turns to Ronaldinho and asks the same question. Ronnie retorts: "When I play football I treat everyone as an equal, I see no ethnic or racial divides. The street urchin from Rio is the same as the superstar from Barcelona." Once again St Peter is impressed and nods.

Next he turns to Beckham and says: "I suppose you are looking for your ball back?

What do you call an England cricketer with 100 runs against his name?

A bowler.

One day, a Spurs fan was walking along the beach and came across an odd-looking bottle. Not being one to ignore tradition, he rubbed it and, much to his surprise, a genie appeared. "For releasing me from the bottle, I will grant you three wishes," said the genie. The man was ecstatic. "But there's a catch," the genie continued. ""For each of your wishes, every Arsenal supporter in the world will receive double what you asked for."

"No problem! I can live with that!" replied the elated man.

"What is your first wish?" asked the genie.

"Well, I've always wanted a Ferrari!" Poof! – a Ferrari appeared in front of the man.

"Now, every Gooner in the world has been given two Ferraris," said the genie. "What is your next wish?"

"I could really use a million dollars," replied the man, and – poof! – one million dollars appeared at his feet.

"Now, every Gooner in the world is two million dollars richer," the genie reminded the man.

"Well, that's okay, as long as I've got my million," replied the Spurs fan.

"And what is your final wish?" asked the genie.

The man thought long and hard before answering: "Well… you know… I've always really wanted to donate a kidney…"

Q. How does Craig Bellamy change a lightbulb?
A. He holds it in the air, and the world revolves around him.

What have General Pinochet and Blackburn Rovers have in common? They both round people up in football stadiums and torture them.

Glenn Hoddle went to the West Brom Xmas party dressed as a pumpkin. Come midnight he still hadn't turned into a coach.

Snow White, Arnold Schwazennegger and Quasimodo are having a conversation.

Snow White says: "Everybody tells me I am the most beautiful woman that man has ever laid his eyes on, but how do I know?"

Arnie says: "I know what you mean. Everybody tells me I am the most muscular, hunky man that has ever lived, but how do I know?"

Quasimodo says "Yes. Everybody tells me I am the most disgusting, despicable, grotesque creature that has ever roamed the earth, but how do I know?"

Snow White says "Let's go and see the wise man!"

So off they go. Snow White goes in first and five minutes later she comes out and says: "It's true. I am the most beautiful woman that any man has ever laid his eyes on."

Arnie goes in and five minutes later he comes out and says: "It's true. I really am the most muscular, hunky man that has ever lived."

Quasimodo goes in and five minutes later he comes out and says: "Who the hell is this Martin Keown character, then?"

"There's always one of my uncles who watches a boxing match with me and says: 'Sure. Ten million dollars. You know, for that kind of money, I'd fight him.' As if someone is going to pay $200 a ticket to see a 57-year-old carpet salesman get hit in the face once and cry."

Larry Miller

One morning, a foursome of men are waiting at the men's tee, while a foursome of ladies are hitting from the ladies' tee.

The ladies really take their time but finally, the last woman is ready to tee off. She hacks it about ten feet, curses, walks over to the ball and hacks it to another ten feet or so. She looks up at the watching men, shrugs and says, "I guess all those f***ing lessons I took this winter didn't help."

One of the men replies, "Now, there's your problem. You should've taken golf lessons instead. But fancy a drink?"

Q. Why do people take an instant dislike to Robbie Savage?
A. It just saves time.

Two kids are playing football in a park in Manchester. Suddenly one of them is attacked by a Rottweiler which clamps its mouth around the kid's neck. The other kid, seeing the danger his pal is in, picks up one of the sticks they were using as a goal post, puts it through the dogs collar, and using all his strength twists it until the dogs neck breaks and his friend is saved. This is all seen by a local newspaper reporter who sees a possible national headline in the incident, and goes over to the kids.

"That was really heroic," he says. "I can see it now: 'Heroic United fan risks life to save best friend.'"

"But I don't follow United" says the kid.

"OK, how about 'Super City Kid fights off rabid rottweiller to save his pal'"?

"But I don't follow City either", says the kid.

"Well who do you support?" asks the reporter.

"Liverpool", he says.

"Even better", says the reporter, "Scouse bastard murders family pet".

White Hart Lane has arguably the best pitch in the Premiership these days. Not entirely surprising, considering all the shit that's been on there in the past.

Three old football fans are in a church, praying for their teams. The first one asks: "Oh Lord, when will England next win the World Cup?"

"God Replies, "In the next five years."

"But I'll be dead by then," says the man.

The second one asks: "Oh Lord, when will Man United next win the European Cup?"

"In the next ten years," replies the Good Lord.

"But I'll be dead by then", says the man.

The third one asks: "Oh Lord, when will Newcastle win the Premiership?"

God answers: "I'll be dead by then!"

A man without a ticket scales the walls of the Millennium Stadium to watch Wigan's first cup final. About five to three he sees spare seat next to an old bloke and asks if it's taken.

"No," says the man, "it was my wife's but she died. We have been season ticket holders for over thirty years and this would have been her first cup final, so sit down you can have the seat."

After a short while the man says to the old bloke: "Did you not have any friends or relative who would have liked your wife's seat?"

"Oh yes," said the old man, "but they all had to go to her funeral."

Why won't Crag Bellamy play cricket? Because he really hates bouncers.

Graeme Souness goes into the local supermarket and sees an old biddy struggling with heavy shopping bags. "Can you manage?" he asks the blue-rinsed old dear.

"No chance!" she replies, "you got yourself in to this mess…"

Hours after the end of the world, a border dispute emerged between Heaven and Hell. God invited the Devil over to discuss how to resolve the dispute. Satan suggests a game of football between Heaven and Hell. God, always fair, says to the devil, "the heat must be affecting your brain, the game will be so one sided! Don't you know all the good players go to heaven?"

"Yeah," replies the devil, smiling, "but we've got all the refs."

A Man City and Man United fan collide in a huge accident on the motorway. Both cars are a wreck, but both men are unhurt.

"This must be a sign from God that we are meant to be friends," says the City fan.

"I agree" replies the United fan.

The City fan then returns to the wreckage of his car, and finds a bottle of whiskey he had been saving. "Look" he says to the United fan, "this must be another sign from God, we should drink this whiskey to celebrate our friendship and survival."

He hands the bottle over to the United fan who takes several large gulp from the bottle before passing it back to the City fan, who then puts the top back on & returns the bottle to his car.

"Aren't you having any?" asks the United fan.

"No" replied the City fan, "I think I'll wait 'til the police get here."

I backed a horse today, at 20 to 1. It came in at 20 past 4.

Tommy Cooper

Q. What's the difference between a Manchester United fan and a vibrator?

A. A Manchester United fan is a *real* dick.

Q. How do you define 144 Chelsea fans?

A. Gross stupidity

Classic Gazza…

Gazza's first training session after his £5million move to Lazio – and career threatening knee injury – has just about every journalist in Italy standing on the sidelines. After a doing couple of gentle laps of the pitch, Gazza suddenly falls to the ground clutching his dodgy knee, screaming in agony and writhing around on the pitch. A deathly silence spreads over the training ground as the club's physios sprint in panic to where the stricken Geordie is laying. When the medics are a few yards away, Gazza jumps up and continues jogging around the pitch without saying a single word…

When asked for a comment whilst playing for Lazio, he burped loudly into a TV microphone. He was fined £39,000.

On the eve of a match against Norway, a Norwegian tv crew asked Gazza if he had a message his opponents. "Fuck off Norway!" he replied, before running off.

When asked to mouth his own name for the BBC's Italia 90 coverage, Gazza chose to mouth "Fucking wanker" instead – which the Beeb duly used for the rest of the tournament.

He booked a course of sun-bed sessions for Tony Cunningham, his Newcastle team mate. Tony Cunningham is black.

Told the president of the Danish FA that he could speak Danish, before doing his best *Muppet Show chef impression*.

Walked into the Middlesbrough canteen and ordered lunch – wearing nothing but a pair of socks. Not long before 'borrowing' the Boro team bus, crashing it in the car park and causing over £300,000-worth of damage…

When asked for his nationality before an operation, Gazza told the nurse: "Church Of England."

On meeting Lazio's president, Sergio Cragnotti, for the first time to discuss his big-money move to the Italian club, his opening gambit was to tell the esteemed businessman how much he reminded him of English comedian Russ Abbot.

On his first night in Rome after joining Lazio, Gazza got away from his minder, left his shoes by an empty window and hid in a cupboard. The poor minder was convinced his charge had killed himself jumping out the window…

He sent a rose to the Wimbledon dressing room for Vinnie Jones following the infamous ball-squeezing incident. And was reputed to have received a toilet brush in return.

Barely an hour after playing for England, he allegedly met showbiz pals Danny Baker and Chris Evans in a Hampstead pub while still wearing his full kit… boots and all!

SHOWBIZ

"The only thing I want to go on is *Deal Or No Deal*. Not a special edition, the normal show. I'll be Simon from Barnsley, see if anyone notices."

Arctic Monkeys drummer Matt Helders on his most showbiz ambition

"Kinder Surprise chocolate eggs: must be bought separately rather than in packs, because it's more likely the toys inside are different."

Highlight of the Motorhead frontman Lemmy's 35-page backstage rider

"The staff in my local Waitrose are really blasé about me now. They'll be like, 'Him? Oh he's in here all the fucking time. And between me and you, he doesn't eat very well.'"

Noel Gallagher on grocery shopping

"I was thieving when I was about 11, before I became an arty c***. We'd run into a sweet shop, grab stuff and fuck off. I was a good little thief."

Danny Dyer on his law-abiding childhood

"I've sponsored a child in Africa. She's got a Jimmy Carr t-shirt, a Jimmy Carr hat. But I worry if it's making any difference. I'm not getting any more bookings."

Jimmy Carr

"When I die, even if I've been knighted, it'll still be: Welsh Toilet Duck man quacks his last quack."

Rob Brydon fears being remembered more for voiceovers than his shows

"If I saw an ugly bird but she was a celebrity with loads of money, she wouldn't attract me at all."

Rio Ferdinand on how star-shagging doesn't work in reverse

Rik Waller is 60 per cent fat. That's the same as a pork scratching.

Ricky Gervais

Sting is always boasting about eight-hour sex marathons with his wife. Imagine how long he'd be able to go if she was a looker.

Jimmy Carr

"I don't like watching myself. Telly makes me look a little overweight and actually I'm an incredibly slender man."

Matt Lucas: good self image

Glastonbury was very wet and muddy. There was trench foot, dysentery, peaches… all the Geldof daughters.

Sean Locke, 8 Out Of 10 Cats

Carol Vorderman is considered the thinking man's crumpet. Presumably by any man who's thinking 'I wouldn't mind shagging some mutton dressed as lamb tonight.'

Angus Deayton, Would I Lie To You?

"I really fancy Coleen. She's so slutty. Am I a dirty old man?"

Chris Moyles admits to "feelings" for Wayne Rooney's fiancée

That new Heineken ad slogan, "Get the head right and the rest will follow." Wasn't that Abi Titmuss's career plan?

Ian Hyland, News Of The World

"He's the least fashion-conscious person I've ever met. Coleen cuts his hair but if she's not about, his mum does it."

Wayne Rooney's biographer Hunter Davies

"I missed the entire Diana concert 'cos I went to the pub with some Diana lookalikes that haven't worked in 10 years. I just thought they needed cheering up."

Alan Cochran

"Harry apologised to his troops for not being with them. I watched the gig and I would have rather been in Iraq."

Jimmy Carr, 8 Out Of 10 Cats

"I Googled myself this morning and got 7,333,600 matches. Everything from me being a god to The Antichrist. Hey, maybe I am The Antichrist"

David Hasselhoff has a search engine-based identity crisis

"People often ask me what it was like working with *Hollyoaks* girls. I say 'It was hard. In fact it was constantly hard for four years.'"

Former soap "star" and Love Island resident Lee Otway

"Where do I see myself in 20 years? Looking like Noel Edmonds"

Justin Lee Collins

"I do charity work now. I get people off drugs. I used to get drugs off people."

Russell Brand

Top Ten Rappers' Real Names

1. Method Man – Cliff Smith
2. Xzibit – Alvin Joyner
3. Ja Rule – Jeffery Atkins
4. Ludacris – Christopher Brian Bridges
5. Common – Lonnie Lynn Jr.
6. MC Hammer – Stanley Kirk Burrell
7. Ol' Dirty Bastard – Russell Jones
8. Ginuwine – Elgin Lumpkin
9. Ice T – Tracy Marrow
10. Snoop Doggy Dogg – Cordazer Calvin Broadus

"What fragrance do I wear? Opium. The one by Yves Saint Laurent obviously"

Pete Doherty heads off the heroin gags

"I demand a takeaway. I'm drunk and it's my right."

Peep Show's *Robert Webb after a few ales*

"David Mitchell's like a walking David Attenbrough documentary. He's got the eyes of a shark, the brain of a dolphin and the flight of a gazelle"

Friday Night Project's *Justin Lee Collins on his posh Peep Show mate*

Hello, I'm Jimmy Carr, I'm one of the biggest faces of British comedy. Literally.

Jimmy Carr

"P. Diddy throws the biggest, but mine are small and potent. I just invite the right people. I'm efficient with my parties."

Jamie Foxx. Maybe he's got no mates

"I met a little girl who has cancer but she's, like, better now because she got to hang out with me. I'm so glad I can touch people's lives like that."

Paris Hilton heals the world

"There are rumours that Nicole Richie is pregnant. Apparently you can tell because she's only throwing up in the morning."

Craig Ferguson, US talkshow host

Top Ten Jobs Pop Stars Did Before They Were Famous

1. Noel Gallagher – baker
2. Ronnie Vannucci (Killers) – wedding photographer
3. Ricky Wilson (Kaiser Chiefs) – art teacher
4. Fergie (Black Eyed Peas) – voice of Sally on Charlie Brown cartoons
5. Nelly – scouted by Atlanta Braves and Pittsburgh pirates to play pro baseball
6. Ice Cube – trainee architectural draftsman
7. Kurt Cobain – Janitor for Lemons Janitorial Services
8. Coolio – fireman
9. Jay-Z – sales clerk at Kennedy Fried Chicken
10. Ozzy Osbourne – abbatoir worker

"We got to the checkout and there's this square thing, and I'm like what's this, guys? They said, 'That's so you can use your credit card'. I was like, 'You can use credit cards in grocery stores now?"

Down-to-earth Janet Jackson visits a supermarket

"There's still a world full of people out there who think there's not much more to me than the girl who can wear tiny tops."

We've no idea what Jennifer Love Hewitt's on about, have you?

"My tattoos are always free, man. I can pretty much walk in anywhere I fancy and they'll do one for free. If they're not, I'm walking out."

Heavily-inked rapper The Game

"If I could change anything about myself, it'd be the heat levels in my body. I blush and people always think I fancy them. Actually I'm just really hot"

TV prankstress Daisy Donovan flushes with success

A cockroach can live for a whole week without a head. Beat that Heather Mills!"

Jimmy Carr

I did a charity gig for cancer last week. If I ever get cancer, I'll be in the ward saying, "See that machine? I paid for it. Now get that little bald fucker off it."

Ricky Gervais

"I still live like a student but with nicer carpets"

Stephen Merchant sums up his post-fame lifestyle

"My wife bought me a pedometer recently. You're meant to take 10,000 steps a day and I did 15,000, just lazing at home. I can't keep still. That's why I'm so thin."

Office-*turned*-Pirates of the Caribbean *star Mackenzie Crook: twitchy*

"I get so much attention for being sexual and beautiful, so I down-play that side of myself."

Lost *star Evangeline Lilly. Anyone else just stopped fancying her?*

"Ms Spears did not vomit on him. He just had peanut butter on his hands."

Britney's publicity people denying she puked all over a new male beau

"I've only ever bought one album – *But Seriously* by Phil Collins. I was 15, decided to get into music, went into WH Smith and that was No. 1, so I assumed it was the best."

David Mitchell from **Peep Show** *on his paltry music collection*

"Sky News, a channel where people don't swear? Fuck that! Fucking nutbag!' Oops, are we live? I do apologise. It was a joke."

Dame Helen Mirren turns the air blue on the Baftas red carpet

"I'm tired of the attention I'm getting from men. I can't go out without someone hitting on me."

Jessica Simpson is already tiring of the single life

"If I was invisible for the day, I'd go over to Bob Geldof's and slap Peaches."

The Friday Night Project's *Alan Carr speaks sense*

"I've had enough of spending £100 an hour on therapy sessions. I thought I might as well get a pair of trainers. It's the best therapy I've ever had. I wish somebody had told me that 12 years ago."

Ronnie O'Sullivan on the powers of shopping

"I'm not a bad person. I genuinely don't want to upset anybody. Off the air, I'm quiet, shy almost."

DJ Chris Moyles insists he's nothing like his loudmouth, radio persona

Jeremy Beadle had a small penis.
   But on the other hand, it was quite big.

"Ricky Gervais tries to fuck you up. He'll fart in the middle of a scene and won't crack a smile."

Kate Winslet recalls her nun episode of Extras

"It's because my nether regions always hang to the left, like an aubergine."

Gordon Ramsay on why he called his first restaurant Aubergine

"All that matters in music today is that your song becomes a ringtone."

Coldplay's Chris Martin hits out at record labels

"Jennifer Aniston goes to Malibu to shout at the sea. I drink Malibu and shout at pigeons.

Bill Bailey

Q. What's the difference between David Beckham and an Airfix kit with no glue?
A. One's a glueless kit…

Q. Why is David Beckham like a Ferrero Rocher?
A. They both come in a posh box.

Q. What's the difference between David Beckham and Posh?
A. Posh doesn't lash out when she's taken from behind.

Victoria and David Beckham are watching the *Six O'Clock News*.

The headline story is about a man who's threatening to jump off a bridge on to the busy road below.

Victoria turns to David and says, "I bet you £10,000 that he jumps."

David says, "£10,000? Done."

The pair shake on it and continue watching.

Sure enough, the man jumps and hits the road below with a thud.

David takes £10,000 out of his pocket and gives it to Victoria.

Victoria says, "I can't take that from you. I was cheating. I saw a news bulletin earlier, so I knew what was going to happen."

David says, "No, babe, the money's yours. I saw the earlier bulletin too; I just didn't think he'd do it again.'"

Q. Why did David Beckham have a skinhead?

A. Because someone told Victoria sex would be better if she shaved her twat.

Camilla goes to her doctor and says, 'When I suck Charles's dick, I get stomach ache.'

The doctor says, 'Have you tried Andrew's?'

Tom Cruise has asked Kelly Holmes on a date.

He would've asked Paula Radcliffe but he wanted a girl who'd go all the way.

Q. How can you pick out Dolly Parton's kids in the playground?

A. They're the ones with stretch marks around their lips.

Q. What's the definition of endless love?

A. Stevie Wonder and Ray Charles playing tennis.

George Michael and Elton John have written a gay version of *The Wizard of Oz*.

It's called *Swallow the Yellow Thick Load*.

Will Young, Robbie Williams and Kylie Minogue enjoy a night on the town together.

After they leave the nightclub, Kylie's drunkenly mucking about when she gets her head stuck between some railings.

Robbie decides to take full advantage of this and lifts up her little skirt, pushes her thong to one side and gives her a good seeing-to.

Robbie says, "That was great. Your turn, Will!"

But Will is crying.

Robbie says, "What's wrong, Will?"

Will sobs, "My head won't fit between the railings."

George Michael was rushed to hospital with a Mars bar stuffed up his backside.

Subsequent tests revealed it was actually a careless Wispa.

Q. What's the difference between Jamie Oliver and a marathon?

A. One's a pant in the country...

Q. Why does John Leslie cry during sex?

A. Pepper spray.

St Peter is standing guard over Heaven when a man approaches, claiming to be Bill Gates.

St Peter asks for proof of identity, so Bill shows his bank balance.

St Peter says, "In you go."

A second man approaches, claiming to be Stephen Hawking. St Peter asks for proof of identity, so Hawking explains the Big Bang Theory.

St Peter says, "In you go."

A third man approaches, claiming to be David Beckham. But when St Peter asks him to prove his identity, Beckham gets annoyed.

St Peter says, "Come on. Even Bill Gates and Stephen Hawking had to do it.'"

Beckham says, "Who?"

St Peter says, "OK, in you go."

Q. Heard about Michael Barrymore's new sitcom?

A. It's called *Only Pools and Corpses*.

Q. Why doesn't Michael Barrymore keep any ashtrays in the house?

A. Because he puts the fags out in the swimming pool.

Q. What do you get if you cross Pete Doherty with Bill Oddie?

A. A quack addict.

Q. What did the Queen buy Camilla for her wedding anniversary?

A. A weekend in Paris and a chauffeur-driven Mercedes.

It's the Sixties, and one night Michael Caine throws a party for all his favourite bands: Led Zeppelin, Deep Purple, the Doors, the Rolling Stones, the Beatles and loads more, together with models, film stars and loads of groupies.

For his special favourites, The Doors, he's arranged a special treat. He gathers the band together and says, "See that yellow door at the end of the corridor? There's a girl in there waiting for you and she wants to suck off all four of you."

Jim Morrison and the guys are excited and charge off to the yellow room. Sure enough, there's a very sexy, very naked rock chick there, and she does indeed proceed to blow all four of them, one at a time.

They rejoin the party satisfied, and Jim tells Mick Jagger what a great time they had. Next thing you know, Mick and the rest of the Rolling Stones pile into the yellow room and the groupie starts to give them the same treatment.

Five minutes later, as she's working on Keith Richards, in bursts Michael Caine.

"What the hell are you doing, girl?" he cries. "You were only supposed to blow the bloody Doors off!"

Q.   Did you go to Rod Hull's funeral?

A.   Apparently the reception was crap.

Victoria Beckham phones the doctor in a panic late one night.

She says, "Doctor, you've got to come over. David's just swallowed a condom."

The doctor rushes to get his things together when the phone rings. It's Victoria again.

She says, "Don't worry, Doc, there's no need to come round. We've found another one."

Snow White, Tom Thumb and Quasimodo are sitting in a pub with their mates.

Snow White says, "There's no doubt about it: I'm the fairest in the land."

Tom Thumb says, "There's no doubt about it: I'm the smallest in the land."

Quasimodo says, "There's no doubt about it: I'm the ugliest in the land."

Their mates tell them to prove it by going to the magic all-knowing mirror.

The three head off.

A few minutes later, the door of the pub bursts open and Snow White runs in and shouts, "It's official – I'm the fairest in the land!'

Shortly afterwards, the door again bursts open and Tom

Thumb runs in and shouts, "It's official – I'm the smallest in the land!"

Five minutes later, the door gets kicked in and Quasimodo stomps through and bellows, "Who the hell is Iain Dowie?"

Q. Have you seen Stevie Wonder's wife lately?
A. Neither has he.

Q. What used to have three legs and live on a farm?
A. The McCartney family.

Q. How did Tommy Cooper die?
A. Just like that.

Q. What's black and sits at the top of the stairs?
A. Stephen Hawking in a house fire.

CHAVS & MORE...

Q. What's the difference between a chav and a coconut?
A. One's thick and hairy, the other's a coconut.

Q. Two chavs jump off Beachy Head. Who wins?
A. Society.

Q. What do you call a chav at college?
A. The cleaner.

Q. Why did the chav cross the road?
A. To start a fight with a random stranger for no reason whatsoever.

Q. What do you call an Eskimo chav?
A. An Innuinnit.

Q. What does a chav girl use as protection during sex?
A. A bus shelter.

Q. What do you call a 30-year-old chav girl?
A. Granny.

Q. What do you call a chav in a box?
A. Innit.

Q. What do you call a chav in a filing cabinet?
A. Sorted.

Q. What do you call a chav in a box with a lock on it?
A. Safe.

Q. What do you say to a chav in a suit?
A. "Will the defendant please stand?"

Q. What do you call a chav girl in a white tracksuit?
A. The bride.

Q. If you see a chav on a bike, why should you try not to hit him?
A. It might be your bike.

Q. What's the first question at a chav quiz night?
A. "What you lookin' at?"

Q. How many chavs does it take to clean a floor?
A. None – dat's some uvver bleeder's job, innit?

Q. Why are chavs like Slinkies?
A. They have no real use but it's great to watch one fall down a flight of stairs.

Q. What's a chav girl's favourite wine?
A. "Aw, go on, take me to Lakeside, please, please, go on, take me…"

Q. Two chavs in a car without any music. Who's driving?
A. The police.

Q. How do you get 100 chavs into a phone box?
A. Paint three stripes on it.

Q. What do you call 100 chavs at the bottom of a river?
A. A start.

A chav walks into the Jobcentre, marches up to the counter and says, "Hi, I'm looking for a job."

The man behind the counter replies, "Well, we've just got a listing from a millionaire who wants a chauffeur/bodyguard for his nymphomaniac daughter. You'll have to drive around in a Mercedes, uniform provided. Because of the long hours, meals will be provided, and you'll also be required to escort the young lady on her holidays. The salary is £200k."

The chav says, "You're bullshitting me!"

The man says, "Well, you started it!"

Q. What do you call a knife in a chav estate?
A. Exhibit A.

The three wise men arrived to visit the child lying in the manger. One of the wise men was exceptionally tall and smacked his head on a low beam as he entered the stable. "Jesus Christ!" he exclaimed.

"Write that down, Mary," said Joseph "It's better than Derek."

popbitch

Q. Where do you take a chav girl for a decent night out?
A. Up the arse.

Q. Why is three chavs going over a cliff in a Nova a shame?
A. A Nova has four seats.

Some chavs are driving through Wales.

As they approach Llanfairpwllgwyngyllgogerychwyrndrobwllll-antysi-liogogogoch, they start arguing about the pronunciation of the town's name.

The row continues until lunchtime.

As they stand at the counter of the local restaurant, one chav says to the blonde serving girl, "Before we order, could you settle an argument for us? Would you please pronounce where we are, very slowly?"

The blonde leans over the counter and says, "Burrrrrrrrrgerrrrrrr Kiiiiing."

Q. What do you call a chav with nine GCSEs?
A. A liar.

Q. Why did the chav take a shower?
A. He didn't mean to; he just forgot to close the Nova's window in the car wash.

Q. What do you say to a chav with a job?
A. "A Big Mac, please."

Q. What's the difference between a chav girl and a chav bloke?
A. A chav girl has a higher sperm count.

What's the difference between your wife and your job?
   After ten years your job still sucks.

Two nuns are driving down a road late at night when a vampire jumps onto the bonnet. The nun who is driving says to the other, "Quick! Show him your cross." So the other nun leans out of the window and shouts, "Get off our fucking car!"

Buddha goes into a pizzeria and says, "Make me one with everything."

A guy sitting at a bar at Heathrow Terminal 3 noticed a really beautiful woman sitting next to him. He thought to himself: "Wow, she's so gorgeous she must be an off duty flight attendant. But which airline does she work for?" Hoping to pick her up, he leaned towards her and uttered the Delta slogan: "Love to fly and it shows?"

She gave him a blank, confused stare and he immediately thought to himself: "Damn, she doesn't work for Delta."

A moment later, another slogan popped into his head. He leaned towards her again, "Something special in the air?"

She gave him the same confused look. He mentally kicked himself, and scratched Singapore Airlines off the list.

Next he tried the Thai Airways slogan: "Smooth as Silk."

This time the woman turned on him, "What the fuck do you want?"

The man smiled, then slumped back in his chair, and said "Ahhhhh, Ryanair!"

How many Jews does it take to screw in a lightbulb?
One, you anti-Semitic piece of shit.

Louis Ramey, stand-up

The seven dwarfs went to the Vatican, and because they are THE DWARFS, they are ushered in to see the Pope. Dopey leads the pack.

"Son," says the Pope, "What can I do for you?"

Dopey replies, "Excuse me, Excellency, but are there any dwarf nuns in Rome?"

The Pope wrinkles his brow at the odd question, thinks for a moment and answers, "No, Dopey, there are no dwarf nuns in Rome."

In the background, a few of the dwarfs start giggling.

Dopey turns around and gives them a glare, silencing them.

Dopey turns back, "Your Worship, are there any dwarf nuns in all of Europe?"

The Pope, puzzled now, again thinks for a moment and then answers, "No, Dopey, there are no dwarf nuns in Europe."

This time, all the other dwarfs burst into laughter.

Once again, Dopey turns around and silences them with an angry glare.

Dopey turns back to the Pope and says, "Mr Pope, are there ANY dwarf nuns anywhere in the world?"

"I'm sorry, my son, there are no dwarf nuns anywhere in the world."

The other dwarfs collapse into a heap, rolling and laughing, pounding the floor, tears rolling down their cheeks as they begin chanting…

"Dopey fucked a penguin!… Dopey fucked a penguin!"

Bloke answers the phone and it's a casualty doctor.

The doctor says, "Your wife was in a serious car accident, and I have bad news and good news. The bad news is, she's lost all use of both arms and both legs, and will need help eating and going to the bathroom for the rest of her life."

Bloke says, "My God. What's the good news?"

The doctor says, "I'm kidding. She's dead."

Two fish swim into a concrete wall. One turns to the other and says: "Dam!"

An old lady dies and goes to heaven. She's chatting it up with St Peter at the Pearly Gates when all of a sudden she hears the most awful, blood curdling screams.

"Don't worry about that," says St Peter, "it's only someone having the holes put into her shoulder blades for wings."

The old lady looks a little uncomfortable but carries on with the conversation. Ten minutes later, there are more blood curdling screams. "Oh my God," says the old lady, "now what's happening?"

"Not to worry," says St Peter, "She's just having her head drilled to fit the halo."

"I can't do this," says the old lady, "I'm going to hell."

"You can't go there," says St. Peter. "You'll be raped and sodomized."

"Maybe so," says the old lady, "but I've already got the holes for that."

So I got a job as the Queen's hairdresser. I parked outside Buckingham Palace and a policeman said to me: "Have you got a permit?"

And I said "No – I've just got to take a bit off the back."

Tim Vine

Why does Snoop Dogg always carry an umbrella?
For drizzle.

A TV reporter goes to a retirement home to interview an aged but legendary explorer. The reporter asked the old man to tell him the most frightening experience he had ever had. The old explorer didn't hesitate:

"Once I was hunting Bengal tigers in the jungles of India. I was on a narrow path and my faithful native gun-bearer was behind me. Suddenly the largest tiger I've ever seen leaped onto the path in front of us. I turned to get my weapon only to find the native had fled. The tiger eapt toward me with a mighty ROARRRR! I soiled myself…"

The reporter said, "Under those circumstances, sir, anyone would have done the same."

The old explorer replies, "No, not then – just now when I went ROARRRR!"

Comedy Central, *US TV show*

Q. What do you call a Scottish cloakroom attendant?

A. Angus McCoatup.

What do you call a woman who knows where her husband is every night?
A widow.

Two Mexicans are stuck in the desert, wandering aimlessly and close to death. They are close to just lying down and waiting for the inevitable, when all of a sudden… "Hey Pepe, do you smell what I smell. Ees bacon I is sure of eet."

"Si, Luis eet smells like bacon to meee."

So, with renewed strength, they struggle up the next sand dune, and there, in the distance, is a tree loaded with bacon. There's raw bacon, dripping with moisture, there's fried bacon, back bacon, double smoked bacon… every imaginable kind of cured pig meat.

"Pepe, Pepe, we is saved. Eees a bacon tree."

"Luis, are you sure ees not a meerage? We ees in the desert don't forget."

"Pepe when deed you ever hear of a meerage that smell like bacon… ees no meerage, ees a bacon tree".

And with that… Luis Races towards the tree. He gets to within 5 metres, Pepe following closely behind, when all of a sudden, a machine gun opens up, and Luis is cut down in his tracks. It is clear he is mortally wounded but, a true friend that he is, he manages to warn Pepe with his dying breath.

"Pepe… go back man, you was right ees not a bacon tree."

"Luis Luis mi amigo… what ees it?

"Pepe… ees not a bacon tree… Ees … Eees a Ham Bush.

Why did the scientist fit his door with an old fashioned knocker?

He wanted to win the no-bell prize.

Innkeeper: "The room is £15 a night. It's £5 if you make your own bed."
Guest: "I'll make my own bed."
Innkeeper: "Good. I'll get you some nails and wood."

This morning on the way to work I rear-ended a car at some lights while not really paying attention. The driver got out and he was a dwarf.

He said, "I'm not happy…"

I replied, "Well, which one are you then?"

popbitch.com

There once was pirate captain who, whenever it looked like a battle would be imminent would change into a red shirt. After observing this behaviour for a few months, one of the crew members asked him what it meant.

"It's in case I get shot. I don't want you crew members to see blood and freak out."

"That's very sensible, sir." At that moment, the crew member spotted eight hostile ships on the horizon. The captain all of a sudden looked very concerned.

"Get my brown pants."

An elderly couple walk into a fast food restaurant. They order one hamburger, one order of fries and one drink.

The old man unwraps the plain hamburger and carefully cuts it in half. He places one half in front of his wife. He then carefully counts out the fries, dividing them into two piles and neatly placing one pile in front of his wife. He takes a sip of the drink, his wife takes a sip and then sets the cup down between them. As he begins to eat his few bites of hamburger, the people around them keep looking over and whispering "That poor old couple – all they can afford is one meal for the two of them."

As the man begins to eat his fries a young man comes to the table. He politely offers to buy another meal for the old couple. The old man replies that they're just fine – they're just used to sharing everything.

The surrounding people noticed the little old lady hadn't eaten a bite. She sits there watching her husband eat and occasionally taking turns sipping the drink.

Again the young man comes over and begs them to let him buy another meal for them.

This time the old woman says "No, thank you, we are used to sharing everything."

As the old man finishes and was wipes his face neatly with the napkin,the young man again comes over to the little old lady who had yet to eata single bite of food and asks "May I ask what is it you are waiting for?"

The old woman answers "The teeth."

Two men bump into each other in an airport. The first man says ' I can't see my wife.'

The second replies 'What a coincidence, I can't find mine either. What does yours look like?'

First man: 'She's 5ft10, blonde, big boobs, mini skirt, stockings, stilettos and a boob tube. What's yours look like?'

Second man says: 'Never mind her, we'll look for yours.'

Daily Star

Q. What do you call a little German who lives in a tin?
A. Heinz.

Q. What has 75 balls and screws old ladies?

A. Bingo.

Good news: Pete Doherty has entered a 12-step programme. Bad news: he lives 12 steps from a crack house.

A guy calls his boss and says, "I can't come in for work today. I'm sick."
The boss said, "How sick are you?"
The guy says, "I'm fucking my cat."

Q. What have Richard Hammond and Pete Doherty got in common?

A. They both do *Top Gear* and have had Moss on their face.

Little Johnny walked in one day on his daddy in the bathroom. He asked his father what that was hanging between his legs. His father replied that it was the perfect penis. The next day at school, Johnny pulled his pants down in front of his classmates.

"What's that?" asked Jenny."

"'Well," said Johnny, "if it was about 3 inches smaller, it would be the perfect penis."

What do you call 100 nuns in a shop? Virgin Megastore

A young couple leave the reception and arrive at the hotel where they're spending their wedding night. The champagne is opened and they start undressing.

As the groom removes his socks, the bride says: "What's wrong with your feet? Your toes look all mangled and weird."

"I had tolio as a child," he replies.

"You mean polio?"

"No, tolio. It only affected my toes."

As he takes off his trousers, his new wife asks: "And what's wrong with your knees? They're all lumpy and deformed."

"As a child I also had kneasles," he replied.

"You mean measles?"

"No, kneasles. It only affected my knees."

She keeps watching as he finally removes his Y-fronts. "Don't tell me," she sighs. "Smallcox?"

Tam Cowan, Daily Record

A bloke offered me a brand new widescreen telly. OK the volume knob was stuck on maximum, but then he only wanted a quid for it. I mean, how could I turn that down?

Tim Vine

Q: Did you hear about the angry fly on the toilet seat?
A: He got pissed off.

Q. How many cool people does it take to screw in a light bulb?
A. What? You don't know?

"For my birthday I got a humidifier and a de-humidifier. I put them in the same room and let them fight it out."

Steven Wright

Two men were changing in the locker room after a game of tennis. One notices the other one is putting on a pair of stockings and suspenders. He says "When did you start wearing them?" To which the other man replies "Since my wife found a pair on the back seat of the car."

Q. Why does Mike Tyson cry during sex?
A. Mace will do that to you.

Q. What did the Mexican fireman name his two sons?
A. Jose and Hose B.

A man goes to the doctor and says, "Doctor, I've got a strawberry stuck up my arse."

The doctor says, "I've got some cream for that."

popbitch.com

Luke Skywalker and Obi-Wan Kenobi are in a Chinese restaurant and Luke's having trouble with his chopsticks. Finally, Obi-Wan says: "Use the forks, Luke."

Apple Computer announced today that it has developed a computer chip that can store and play music in a woman's breast implants. The iBreast will cost £499. It's considered to be a major breakthrough because women are always complaining about men staring at their breasts and not listening to them.

The Sun

What do you call someone who covers his genitals in chickpeas and garlic?
A hummusexual

A woman walks into Specsavers to return a pair of glasses that she'd purchased for her husband a week before.

The assistant says, "What seems to be the problem, madam?"

"I'm returning these glasses I bought for my husband", she says, "He's still not seeing things my way."

popbitch.com

A Frenchman, a German and a hypochondriac arrive at a hotel. "I'm tired and thirsty", says the Frenchman. "I must have wine!"

"I'm tired and thirsty," says the German. "I must have beer!"

"I'm tired and thirsty," says the hypochondriac. "I must have diabetes."

The Guardian

How do you get a granny to shout "Fuck"?
Get another to shout "Bingo"

Monica Lewinsky is looking in a mirror. Her frustration over her lack of ability to lose weight was depressing her. In an act of desperation, she decides to call on God for help. "God, if you take away my love handles, I'll devote my life to you," she prays.

And just like that, her ears fell off.

How does Bob Marley like his doughnuts?
Wi' jammin'.

Peter Kay

What did Britney's right leg say to her left leg?
Nothing, they've never been seen together.

Did you hear about Vanessa Feltz getting arrested at customs?
She was trying to smuggle 40lbs of crack in her knickers.

A chav girl goes to the doctors complaining of a weird green rash on her inner thighs. The doctor take one look and says "Tell your boyfriend his gold earrings are fake."

Why does Dr Pepper come in a bottle?
Because his wife's dead.

POLITICS

"Hitler was a bad man. Winston Churchill was a good man. But if you were in a hot-air balloon with Hitler and Churchill, and you were losing altitude…"

Harry Hill

Gordon Brown and George Bush are sitting in a pub with George's dog having a drink.

A man walks in lifts up the dogs tail, shrugs and then walks out again.

Then another man does the same and then another. When a fourth man does it, George stops him and says "You're the fourth person to do this. Why do people keep lifting his tail and having a look?"

To which the man replies, "There is a man outside telling people that there is a dog in here with two arseholes."

"You can't bomb the Afghans back to the Stone Age. They'll go, 'Hey – upgrade!'"

Robin Williams

"President Bush is in Europe preparing for the G8 Summit and he's very excited. He thinks it's a conference on vegetable juice."

David Letterman, The Late Show

"As you know, Saddam Hussein was hung. Or that's what he'd like to tell the ladies."

Jay Leno

D'ohval Office

Top 10 reasons why I, Homer Simpson, should be the next President

10. I'm smarter than the last guy.
9. With an oval office, I can't bump into anything.
8. Fox News is already on my side.
7. I will take full advantage of the free food that comes with the job.
6. I have enormous experience in apologizing for failed decisions.
5. I will appoint a Secretary of Donuts.
4. I will be the Secretary of Donuts.
3. My middle name isn't Hussein… anymore.
2. My vice-president will be Mayor McCheese.
1. Kick-ass inauguration party! Bring a six pack and you're in *Late Night With David Letterman*

"President Bush met with the Pope on Saturday. There was one awkward moment … when he asked the pope, 'Hey, how's Mrs. Pope?'"

Jay Leno

"Man, I'd kill for a Nobel Peace Prize."

Steven Wright

"You wanna know something? I actually like George W Bush. In some ways, I'm the George W. Bush of hip hop – nobody likes me, but I'm still gonna run it for the next four years."

50 Cent

"Pol Pot rounded up everyone who was intellectual and had them killed. And he could tell if they were intellectual by whether they wore glasses. If they're that clever, take them off when you see him coming."

Ricky Gervais

"Bill Clinton earned more than $10 million last year from giving speeches but says he gave half of it to charity. He gives the other half to her sister, Tiffany."

Conan O'Brien, US Talkshow host

While having tea with the Queen, George Bush asked how she makes sure she's surrounded by smart people. "I ask the right questions," she says. With that she phones Tony Blair and says, "Please answer this: your mother has a child, and your father has a child, and this child is not your brother or sister. Who is it?" Tony Blair responds, "It's me, ma'am." Bush returns to Washington and summons Dick Cheney. "Er, your mother has a child, your father has a child, and this child is not your brother or your sister. Who is it?" "Can I get back to you?" asks Cheney and leaves puzzled. In desperation, he calls Colin Powell for help. Powell answers immediately, "It's me, of course." Cheney rushes back to the White House, finds George Bush, and exclaims, "I know the answer, sir! I know who it is! It's Colin Powell!" And Bush replies in disgust, "Wrong, you dumb shit, it's Tony Blair!"

"George W. Bush? Some men are born great. Some achieve greatness. And some get it as a graduation gift."

Robin Williams

"The right to bear arms is slightly less ludicrous than the right to arm bears."

Chris Addison, stand-up

"At the final cabinet meeting Jack Straw told Tony Blair that he'd always be remembered for Northern Ireland, the 2012 Olympics and civil partnership. So presumably if you're a gay sprinter from Belfast he's the best Prime Minister ever."

Trevor McDonald

"It's our president's birthday. He's 61 today. Also, Sylvester Stallone is 61 today. But Stallone and Bush don't have much in common. One's a bad actor who mumbles and blows stuff up, and the other is Sylvester Stallone."

Craig Ferguson

Earlier this week, police defused a potentially massive car bomb parked in front of London's famed Piccadilly Circus. President Bush got a little confused. He called the new prime minister and made sure all the animals and clowns were safe.

Jay Leno, US talkshow host

"I have too many bedrooms and feel bad about it. But not so bad that I'm prepared to let homeless people come and live with me."

The politically correct Steve Coogan

"I couldn't run for office. I've slept with far too many people."

George Clooney dismisses dabbling in politics

"I stand by this man because he stands for things.
Not only for things, he stands on things. Things like aircraft carriers, and rubble, and recently flooded city squares.
And that sends a strong message that no matter what happens to America she will always rebound with the most powerfully staged photo-ops in the world."

US Comedian Stephen Colbert,

Cats can get passports now. How do you think that makes Mohamed Al Fayed feel?

Jeff Green

Ex-President Jimmy Carter said George W. Bush is the worst President in history. But Bush hit back with, "No, that's not true. I was the worst in Maths and English as well."

Jay Leno

News has filtered out that US forces have swooped on an Iraqi primary school and detained teacher Mohammed Al-Hazar. When arrested, Al-Hazar had a ruler, protractor, set square and calculator. George W. Bush says this is clear evidence that Iraq does indeed have weapons of maths instruction.

"John Prescott. A man who couldn't wear a tie and a belt on the same day or he'd turn into sausages."

Frankie Boyle

"People think it'll be all lovely summers and mild winters. Let's see how much they like it when their grandchildren have to live under the sea and start developing gills"

Russell Brand on global warming

Tony Blair and his driver are on their way to Chequers and pass a farm.

Suddenly, a pig jumps out into the middle of the road.

The driver tries to swerve out of the way, but hits him.

He goes to the farmhouse to explain what's happened.

Ten minutes later, he returns to the car holding a beer and a cigar.

Blair notices this and says, "What on earth did you tell them?'"

The driver says, "I told them that I'm Tony Blair's driver and I just killed the pig."

After Yassar Arafat died, the Palestinian undertakers clothed his body in a Newcastle shirt, Spurs shorts and Rangers socks. In his will he'd said he wanted to be buried in the Gaza strip.

Tony Blair is out jogging and accidentally falls into a river.

Three boys see the accident.

Without a second thought, they jump into the water and drag out the soaking Blair.

Blair says, "Boys, you saved my life and deserve a reward. You name it; I'll give it to you."

The first boy says, "I'd like a ticket to Disneyland."

Blair says, "Certainly."

The second boy says, "I'd like an MP3 player."

Blair says, "No problem."

The third boy says, "And I'd like a wheelchair with a stereo in it."

Blair says, "But you're not handicapped."

The boy says, "No, but I will be when my dad finds out I saved you from drowning."

Tony and Cherie Blair are at a restaurant. The waiter tells them that tonight's special is chicken amandine and fresh fish.

Cherie says, "The chicken sounds good; I'll have that."

The waiter says, "Certainly, madam. And the vegetable?" Cherie says, "Oh, he'll have the fish."

Q. Why doesn't Osama Bin Laden have sex and driving lessons on the same day?

A. The camel can't manage it.

George W Bush has a heart attack and dies. He immediately goes to Hell, where the Devil is waiting for him.

The Devil says, "I don't know what to do. You're on my list, but I have no room for you. Tell you what: I've got some people here who weren't quite as bad as you. I'll let one of them go, but you have to take their place. I'll even let you decide who you swap with."

The Devil leads Bush to a series of doors and opens the first. Inside is Ronald Reagan and a large pool of water. Reagan keeps diving in and surfacing, over and over again. Such is his fate in Hell.

Bush says, "No, I don't want to do that. I'm not a good swimmer, so I don't think I could do that all day long."

The Devil leads him to the next room. Inside is Richard Nixon with a sledgehammer and a huge pile of rocks. All he does is swing the hammer, time after time after time.

Bush says, "No; I've got a problem with my shoulder. I'd be in constant agony if all I did was break rocks all day."

The Devil opens a third door. Inside, Bush sees Bill Clinton, lying on the floor with his arms tied behind his head, and his legs spreadeagled. Bent over him is Monica Lewinsky, doing what she does best.

Bush stares in disbelief and says, "Yeah, I can handle this."

The Devil smiles and says, "OK, Monica, you're free to go."

**Q. What's 12 inches long and
 dangles in front of an arsehole?
A. Tony Blair's tie.**

On his birthday, George W Bush comes down to breakfast to find his wife holding a blindfold. She says she has a surprise and blindfolds him. She sits him in a chair at the kitchen table, just as a man tells her she has a call. She tells Bush not to take off the blindfold, as she'll be right back.

As Bush is waiting, and since his wife isn't there to see him, he decides to masturbate to pass the time.

He pulls down his pants and starts jerking off. He moans in pleasure and makes other noises, but his wife doesn't hear him. Then he hears his wife's footsteps approaching.

He tucks his cock into his pants and wipes his hands on his trousers, just before she enters the room.

His wife says, "OK, you can take your blindfold off."

Bush takes the blindfold off and sees a group of people at the table.

His wife says, "The networks are filming your birthday, live on every channel!"

George W. Bush strides into a library and shouts, "Hi, ma'am! I'd like a burger and fries please!"

The librarian says, "For fuck's sake, you idiot, this is a library!"

"Sorry," says Bush, and whispers, "I'd like a burger and fries, please."

A bloke walks into a bar and says to the bartender, "Isn't that George W Bush and Colin Powell sitting over there?"
The bartender says, "Yep, that's them."

So the bloke walks over to them and says, "Wow, this is a real honour. What are you guys doing in here?"

Bush says, "We're planning World War Three."

The bloke says, "Really? What's going to happen?"

Bush says, "Well, this time we're going to kill 50 million Arabs and one bicycle repairman."

The bloke cries, "A bicycle repairman? Why kill a bicycle repairman?"

Bush turns to Powell and says, "See, dummy! I told you no one would worry about the 50 million Arabs!"

Harold Shipman died after being found hanged in his cell. A prison spokesman said that the killer doctor had simply run out of patients.

A man is driving home from work and notices there is a lot more traffic than normal. Eventually, all the cars grind to a halt. He sees a policeman walking towards his car, so he asks him what's wrong.

The policeman says, "It's a crisis. Gordon Brown is sitting in the road very upset. He doesn't have the £10 billion needed to fill the black hole in his budget, and everyone hates him. He's threatening to douse himself in petrol and set himself on fire."

The bloke says, "What are you doing about it?"

The policeman says, "I'm going car-to-car asking for donations"

The man says, "How much do you have so far?"

The policeman says, "So far, only 99 litres, but a lot of people are still siphoning as we speak."

Prince Charles is driving around the Queen's estate when he accidentally runs over her favourite corgi.

He gets out of his car and sit down on the grass, distraught. His mother will be furious.

Suddenly, he notices a lamp half-buried in the ground.

He digs it up, polishes it and immediately a genie appears.

The genie says, "You have freed me from thousands of years of imprisonment. As a reward, I shall grant you one wish."

Charles says, "I have all the material things I need, but do you think you could bring this dog back to life?'"

The genie looks at the splattered remains and shakes his head.

He says, "You ask too much. The body is too far gone. Its bones are crushed and its brains are splashed all over the road. Even I couldn't bring it back to life. Is there something else you'd like?"

Charles reaches into his pocket and pulls out two photos.

He shows the genie the first photo and says, "I was married to this beautiful woman called Diana." Then he shows the genie the second photo and says, "But now I'm married to this woman called Camilla. Do you think you can make her as beautiful as Diana?"

The genie studies the two photographs and says, "Let's have another look at that dog."

The government today announced that it's changing its emblem to a condom because it more accurately reflects its political stance.

A condom allows for inflation, halts production, destroys the next generation, protects a bunch of pricks and gives you a sense of security while you're actually being screwed.

Tony Blair, Jacques Chirac and George W. Bush are set to face a firing squad in a small Central American country.
Blair is the first one placed against the wall, but he has a cunning plan.

Just before the order to shoot is given, he yells, "Earthquake!"

The firing squad looks round in a panic, while Blair vaults over the wall and escapes.

Chirac is the second one placed against the wall.

The squad is reassembled, but Chirac has been inspired by Blair's getaway.

So before the order to shoot is given, Chirac yells, "Tornado!'"

Again the squad is distracted, and Chirac escapes over the wall.

Finally, Bush is placed against the wall.

He thinks, "I see the pattern here. You just scream out something to alarm everyone, then hop over the wall.'"

So as the rifles are raised in his direction, Bush grins from ear to ear and yells, "Fire!'"

Q. Why was John Paul II cremated?
A. Because the Vatican wanted to use his ashes as Pope-pourri.

Before his inauguration, George W. Bush was invited on a tour of the White House by his predecessor Bill Clinton. After drinking several glasses of iced tea, he asked Clinton if he could use his personal bathroom. Once inside, he was astonished to see that Clinton had a solid gold urinal. That afternoon, Bush told his wife Laura about the urinal.

He said, "Just think. When I'm President, I'll have my own personal gold urinal."

Later, when Laura had lunch with Hillary Clinton, she told her how impressed George had been by the fact that Bill had a gold urinal.

That evening, Bill and Hillary were getting ready for bed. Hillary said, "Well, I found out who pissed in your saxophone."

A bloke goes into a sex shop and asks for an inflatable doll.

The man behind the counter says, "Normal or Palestinian?"

The customer says, "What's the difference?"

The man behind the counter says, "The Palestinian one blows itself up."

An office worker is so frustrated at being passed over for promotion year after year that he goes to a brain-transplant centre in the hope of adding 20 points to his IQ.

The surgeon says, "This is an expensive operation. An ounce of doctor's brain, for example, costs £1,000. An ounce of accountant's brain costs £2,000. An ounce of lawyer's brain is £50,000. And an ounce of Labour MP's brain is £100,000."

The office worker says, "All that money, just for an ounce of Labour MP's brain? Why on earth is that?"

The surgeon says, "Do you have any idea how many Labour MPs we would have to kill?"

Q.   Why does Laura Bush have to go on top?
A.   Because George W. Bush always fucks up.

A man dies and goes to heaven. As he stands in front of St Peter at the Pearly Gates, he sees a huge wall of clocks behind him. He says, "What are all those clocks?"

St Peter says, "Those are Lie Clocks. Everyone on Earth has a Lie Clock. Every time you lie, the hands on your clock will move."

The man says, "Oh. Whose clock is that?"

St Peter says, "That's Mother Teresa's. The hands never moved, indicating that she never told a lie."

The man says, "Incredible. And whose clock is that one?"

St Peter says, "That's Abraham Lincoln's clock. The hands moved twice, telling us that Lincoln told only two lies in his entire life."

The man says, "Where's George W. Bush's clock?"

St Peter says, "In Jesus's office. He's using it as a ceiling fan."

George W. Bush, the Pope and a little boy are on the same plane.

Suddenly the engines fail and the captain says, "We're going to crash. Grab a parachute and escape while you can."

The three of them rush over to the parachutes – but find there are only two.

Bush grabs one, opens the door and jumps out, shouting, "I'm too important to die!"

The Pope and the little boy look at each other.

The Pope says, "Little boy, I've had a good long life and I'm sure I'll be going to a better place. You take the parachute."

The little boy says, "It's OK, you have it – and I'll have the second one. That tit Bush took my rucksack."

At the Royal wedding, Camilla was in agony: her shoes were way too small.

When she and Charles got to the bridal suite, the only thing she could think of was getting her shoes off.

The rest of the Royal Family crowded round the bedroom door and heard what they expected: grunts and straining noises.

Eventually they heard Charles say, "My, that was tight.'"

The Queen whispered, "Told you Camilla was a virgin.'"

Then, to their surprise, they heard Charles say, "Right. Now for the other one."

There followed more grunting, until Charles said, "My God! That was even tighter!"

"That's my boy," said the Duke. "Once a sailor, always a sailor!"

The Queen is visiting one of London's top hospitals and she says she wants to see absolutely everything.

During her tour, she passes a room where a male patient is masturbating.

The Queen says, "Oh my, that's disgraceful. What's the meaning of this?"

The doctor leading the tour says, "I'm sorry, your Majesty, but this man has a very serious medical condition and is only following doctor's orders. His body produces too much semen and his testicles keep overfilling. Until we can find out exactly what's causing this problem, he's been instructed to do this at least five times a day or there's a danger that his testicles will explode, killing him instantly."

The Queen says, "Oh, I am sorry."

On the next floor, they pass a room where a young nurse is giving a patient a blow-job.

The Queen says, "Oh my, what's happening in there?"

The doctor says, "Same problem, but he's with BUPA."

Q. Why shouldn't you wear Y-fronts in Ukraine?
A. Chernobyl fallout.

George W Bush visits a school to deliver a basic talk on Greek literature.

He sits in front of the class and says, "Who knows what a tragedy is?"

A small boy says, "Say my friend got run over by a tractor and died. Would that be a tragedy?"

Bush says, "No, that's not a tragedy – that would be an accident."

A small girl says, "Is it when a bus of little children crashes and they die?"

Bush says, "No, but it would be a great loss."

Another boy says, "Would a tragedy be if Air Force One was shot down and you died?"

Bush says, "Why do you say that?"

The boy says, "Because it wouldn't be an accident and it certainly wouldn't be a great loss."

Q. What's al-Qaeda's favourite drink?
A. Osama Bin Latte.

PUB JOKES

Two blokes are in the pub. One says to the other, "Your round."

The other replies, "So are you, you fat bastard."

A gorgeous woman wanders over to the bar in a pub. She seductively signals at the barman to bring his face close to hers, then reaches out her hands and caresses his beard.

"Are you the manager"' she purrs, stroking his face.

"No," he replies, wide-eyed.

"Can you get him for me?" she whispers, running her hands through his hair.

"I'm afraid I can't," he breathes, clearly aroused. "Is there anything I can do?"

"Yes," she continues huskily, popping a couple of fingers into his mouth for him to suck. "Tell him there's no loo paper or soap in the ladies' toilets."

> **"Someone asked me if I always drink whisky neat, I said, 'No – sometimes my shirt's hanging out.'"**
>
> *Tommy Cooper*

A white horse walks into a bar.

Barman says: "We've got a whisky named after you."
Horse goes, "What, Dave?"

A man walks into a pub, goes up to the bar. As he orders his drink, a voice from the bowl of peanuts on the bar goes, "Like your shirt mate." Before he can react, he hears from the direction of the cigarette machine, "Never mind your shirt, you're an ugly bastard. "What the hell's going on?" he asks the barman. "Ah, well the peanuts are complementary but the cigarette machine's out of order."

Bloke's walking past a pub and sees a sign: "Pies 50p, handjobs £1."

He goes in and sees the most gorgeous barmaid. He says, "Are you the one who gives handjobs for a quid?"

"Yep," she says.

"Well wash your hands then, I want a pie."

> **"There's these machines now that tell you when to stop drinking... Cashpoint machines."**
>
> *Harry Hill*

A woman walks into a bar and asks for a double entendre. So the barman gives her one.

A bra and a set of jump leads walk into a pub. The barman says to the bra, "I'm not serving you lot. You're off your tits and your mates look like they want to start something."

A skeleton walks into a pub: "Pint of lager, please barman. Oh, and a mop."

A married couple are discussing the best way to tighten their belts.

Margaret says: "For a start, you spend £20 a week on beer, so that'll stop."

John: "Wait a minute, you spend £30 on make-up and beauty products."

Margaret: "Yes, dear, but that's to make me look attractive."

John: "And what do you think the beer's for?"

William Shakespeare goes into a pub.
The landlord says "Get out, you're bard."

Why are women like pub loos?
They're either vacant, engaged or full of crap.

A hat and a turd go up to the bar but the barman won't serve them. "No way – you're off your head and he's steaming."

A polar bear walks into a pub. Goes up to the bar and says, "Pint of Guinness please… … … and some dry roasted peanuts." Barman replies, "Why the big pause?" "Because I'm a polar bear."

A man runs into a pub and orders the three most expensive malt whiskys they have. The barman lines them up, but before he's finished pouring the third, the bloke downs the first in one. As he necks the second, the barman says to him, "You're in a hurry." The bloke replies, "You would be too if you had what I have. "The barman says, "Oh, sorry to hear that mate, what have you got?" The bloke downs the final whisky and replies, "50p."

An Englishman, Scotsman and Irishman walk into a pub. The barman says, "What is this, some kind of joke?"

Three blind mice walk into a pub. But they are all unaware of their surroundings, so to derive humour from it would be exploitative

Bill Bailey

Bloke goes into the pub and asks for a pint
The barman says, "Sure, that'll be a penny."
Bloke goes, "A penny? This is the cheapest pub in the world! OK, I'll have steak and chips as well."
Barman says, "Very good, sir. That'll be two pence."
Bloke goes, "You're joking! Where's the landlord?"
Barman says, "Upstairs, with my wife."
Bloke says, "What's he doing up there?"
Barman says, "Same as I'm doing to his business."

A hotel mini-bar allows you to see into the future... and what a can of Pepsi will cost in 2020.

Rich Hall

A bloke comes home from the pub one night with a duck under his arm.

He tells his wife, "This is the pig I've been shagging."

His wife goes, "That's a duck."

The bloke goes, "I was talking to the duck."

My local's rough as anything. I went to the pub quiz the other night.

First question was "What the fuck are you looking at?"

Jack Dee

A bloke goes to the pub to meet his mate.

He says, "Sorry I haven't been in touch for a few days – I've been in the hospital getting a dirty great mole removed from the end of my cock."

His mate says, "Sounds painful."

He says, "Too right – that's the last time I shag one of those little buggers."

ANIMALS

Q. Why were men given larger brains than dogs?
A. So they wouldn't hump women's legs at parties.

A cowboy is taken prisoner by a group of Red Indians. The Indians are ready to kill him when the chief announces that because of the Celebration of the Great Spirit, they'll grant the cowboy three wishes before he dies.

The chief says, "What do you want for your first wish?"

The cowboy says, "I want to talk to my horse."

So he goes over to his horse and whispers in its ear.

The horse neighs and takes off at speed.

About an hour later, it returns with a naked lady on its back.

The chief says, "What do you want for your second wish?"

The cowboy says, "I want to talk to my horse again."

So again he whispers in the horse's ear. The horse neighs and takes off at speed.

About an hour later, the horse comes back with another naked lady on its back.

Then the chief says, "What do you want for your last wish?" The cowboy says, "I want to talk to my horse again.

He grabs the horse by the ears and yells, "You stupid animal: I said 'Posse!'"

Q. Why did the man cross the road?
A. He heard the chicken was a slut.

Q. How does a Welshman improve his girlfriend's taste?
A. By adding mint sauce.

A man goes to his doctor and says, "Doctor, I've just been raped by an elephant. My arsehole has been stretched this wide."

The doctor says, "Bend over and let me have a look."

The bloke bends over and sure enough, his arsehole is about 10 inches across.

"But I thought an elephant's cock was long and thin?" says the doctor.

"Yes, it was," says the man, "but the bastard fingered me first."

Mummy takes little Johnny to the zoo. At the elephant enclosure, the elephant has an erection.

"What's that?" asks little Johnny.

"It's nothing," says the embarrassed mother.

A week later, Johnny's dad takes him and the same thing happens.

"What's that?" asks Johnny.

"A 24-inch penis," replies dad.

"Mummy said it was nothing," says Johnny.

His dad says, "Well, son, your mother's spoilt."

Q. What did the elephant say to the naked man?
A. "How do you breathe through something so small?"

Two blokes are walking through the jungle when the first is bitten on the penis by a snake.

Quickly, the second bloke rings the emergency services on his mobile.

"My friend's been bitten by a snake," he cries. "What can I do?"

The operator says, "Is it a poisonous snake?"

"Yes, a tiger snake," says the second bloke.

"Then you must immediately suck the poison out, or your friend will be dead within an hour."

The second bloke hangs up and says, "Sorry, mate – he says you'll be dead within an hour."

Q. How does a Welshman find a sheep in long grass?
A. Irresistible.

Where would you find an elephant with no legs?

Where you left it.

A bloke goes into a brothel with a tenner.

"Sorry, mate," says the pimp, "the only thing you can have for a tenner is a goat."

The bloke shrugs, pays his money and shags the goat.

The next week he returns to the brothel – but this time he's only got a fiver.

"Sorry," says the pimp, "but all you can get for a fiver is a peep show."

So he goes into the peep show and there's a load of blokes spying on a guy wanking off a gorilla.

"Jesus," says the first bloke. "I've never seen anything like this before."

"You should have been here last week," says the bloke next to him. "There was a guy in there shagging a goat."

"Bullfighters should be made to go in drunk, without a sword and just wearing one of those Viking helmets that people wear. That's a fair fight."

Ricky Gervais on making bloodsports less cruel – to the animals, anyway.

An old lady kept two pet monkeys for years. Eventually one of them died, then two days later the other passed away from grief.

Because they'd been such great companions the old lady took them to be stuffed

The taxidermist asked, "Would you like them mounted?"

"No, no. Holding hands will be fine."

Q.   What's got two legs and bleeds?
A.   Half a dog.

I saw this bloke chatting up a cheetah, I thought "he's trying to pull a fast one".

Peter Kay

A penguin takes his car to a mechanic because there's a funny noise coming from under the bonnet.

"Leave it with me," says the mechanic. "Come back in 20 minutes."

So off goes the penguin. It's a pretty hot day, so on spotting an ice cream van, he goes and buys himself a 99. Now, penguins aren't very good at eating ice creams – the lack of opposable thumbs makes it tricky. So by the time the penguin has finished his 99, he is completely covered in ice cream. It is all over his beak and all over his flippers. Feeling a little sticky, he goes back to the garage.

"Oh, hello," says the mechanic, wiping his hands on a cloth.

"Hello," replies the penguin. "Was it anything serious?"

"Not really, but it looks like you've blown a seal."

"Oh no!" says the penguin, wiping his beak. "It's just ice cream."

A war veteran's walking along the street, dragging his left foot behind him, when he encounters a man coming the other way, doing the same. The first guy nods knowingly, points to his gammy leg and says, "Falklands, 25 years ago."

The other guy replies, "Dog shit, 30 yards back there."

"If you're being chased by a police dog, try not to go through a tunnel, then on to a little seesaw, then jump through a hoop of fire. They're trained for that."

Milton Jones

What's do you do if an elephant comes through your window? Swim

A waiter asks a man, "May I take your order, sir?"

"Yes," the man replies. "I'm just wondering, exactly how do you prepare your chickens?"

"Nothing special, sir. We just tell them straight out that they're going to die."

"Animal testing is a terrible idea. They get all nervous and give the wrong answers."

Stephen Fry

Always keen on owning an unusual pet, a man buys what's advertised as a talking centipede from his local pet shop. After paying £5,000, he takes it home in its little box and puts it on top of the mantelpiece. Later that night he taps the box, slides it open and says: "Fancy coming down the pub for a pint?" The centipede doesn't answer. Raising his voice a little, he repeats the question. Still no answer. Convinced he's been conned out of £5000, he angrily shouts: "Fancy coming down the pub for a pint?" The centipede sticks its head out and says: "I heard you the first time. I was putting my fucking shoes on."

Q. What's the difference between a dog and a fox?
A. About five pints

What do you call a bin bag full of mutilated laboratory monkeys?
Rhesus Pieces

Comedy Central, US TV show

The chicken and the egg are laying in bed.

The chicken's smoking a cigarette with a big satisfied smile on its face, while the egg is frowning and looking slightly annoyed.

The egg mutters, "Well, I guess that answers that riddle".

Q. What's the only animal with an arsehole in the middle of its back?
A. A police horse.

Q. What's a shih-tzu?
A. One with no animals.

Q. What do you do if a kitten spits at you?
A. Turn the grill down.

There was magician on a cruise ship and he was really good. He was performing the highlight of his show when a parrot walked onstage and squawked, "It's in his sleeve!" The audience booed and the annoyed magician chased the bird away.

Next night, the magician was performing his highlight again, but in front of a smaller audience. The parrot walked onstage and declared, "It's in his pocket!" The audience again booed and the furious magician chased the bird away.

The next night, as he was again performing his climactic trick, but to a tiny audience. On the lookout this time, the magician saw the parrot in the crowd. But before the parrot could ruin the trick, the boat crashed into a rock and sank.

The magician was lucky enough to find a board to hang on to. On the other end of the board was the parrot. They stared at each other for three full days, neither of them saying anything, when suddenly the parrot said, "OK, I give up. What'd you do with the ship?"

So I said "Do you fancy a game of darts?"
He said "OK then."
I said "Nearest to bull starts."
He said "Baa."
I said "Moo."
He said "You're closest."

Peter Kay

What's got two grey legs and two brown legs?
An elephant with diarrhoea

The police stop a car because the driver has 20 penguins in the back.

"You can't be driving around with a car-load of penguins," says the copper, "Take them to the zoo." The driver agrees.

The following day, the copper spots the same car – and again he has 20 penguins in the back.

"I thought I told you to take those to the zoo," says the policeman.

"I did," said the driver, "and today I'm taking them to the cinema."

What's got four legs and goes "Boo"? A cow with a cold.

A dog goes into a hardware store and says, "I'd like a job, please."

The shop owner says, "We don't hire dogs. Why don't you join the circus?"

The dog says, "What would the circus want with a plumber?"

"People say dogs aren't clever. But when did you see one tread in human shit?"

Billy Connolly

DUMB AND DUMBER

"Don't you know lighting a cigarette the wrong way and inhaling stops the blood flowing to your private parts? And doing it more than once means you may never have an orgasm again."

Paris Hilton's latest flash of genius

"Say Laura, do you think I ought to sing something?"

George W. Bush to his wife, at a Bono-led charity concert

"The phone was ringing. I picked it up, and said 'Who's speaking please?' And a voice said, 'You are.'"

Tim Vine

"Years ago I saw an attractive girl at a bus stop who looked like an effeminate boy I went to school with. I thought he must've had a sex change, so I said "Hello Graham" – it wasn't Graham. The poor girl was mortified."

Richard Madeley's most embarrassing moment

"I tried to rob a department store… with a pricing gun. I said, 'Give me all the money, or I'm marking down everything in the store.'"

Steven Wright

"The next thing I knew, someone was waking me up saying, 'Mr Vegas, maybe you should get dressed.' I was in the hotel reception, naked from the waist down."

Johnny Vegas on a Guinness-fuelled escapade

"One in five people in the world is Chinese. And there are five people in my family, so it must be one of them. It's either my mum or my dad. Or my older brother Colin. Or my younger brother Ho Chan Chu. But I think it's Colin."

Tim Vine

"I go to lots of overseas places, like Canada."

Britney Spears

"I went up to the airport information desk. I said, How many airports are there in the world?"

Jimmy Carr

"I saw this sign on the Underground next to the escalator saying: Dogs Must Be Carried. Could I find a dog anywhere? Could I fuck."

Dave Spikey

"My dad used to say, 'Always fight fire with fire'. Which is probably why he was thrown out of the fire brigade."

Harry Hill

"Most dentists' chairs go up and down. The one I was in went backwards and forwards. I thought, 'This is unusual.' And the dentist said to me, 'Mr Vine, get out of the filing cabinet.'"

Tim Vine

Real Madrid are taking on an AC Milan all star team, but every time George Weah – playing for the Milanese – gets the ball, David Beckham runs up to him, puts his finger to his lips and says, "Shhhhh!" before falling about laughing.

Again, Weah gets the ball, and again, Becks trots up, puts his finger to his lips and goes, "Shhhh…" before giggling to himself like a girl.

After he goes, "Shhh…" for the tenth time, Zidane comes up to the dopey midfielder, looks him in the eye and says, "For fuck's sake, Daveeed, he's a *Liberian*."

"I walked into HMV the other day, and asked the assistant, 'Do you have anything by The Doors?'"
'Yes,' he said. 'Two buckets and a fire extinguisher.'"

Tim Vine

"My most embarrassing moment was once when I showed a holiday video to my entire family and forgot there was a point where I flashed. I only realised a second before it happened and couldn't get to the remote in time. My sister screamed and my mum said: 'Ooh, that's changed.'"

Simon Pegg relives a post-holiday trauma

"DisneyWorld in Florida is my favourite place. I fucking love Mickey Mouse and every time I see the Cinderella Castle, it's my dream. I'd love to live there."

Paul Gascoigne

"I stopped a man from Wigan in the street on the way to the football and I asked him, 'How do you get to the JJB stadium?' And he said, 'Me brother takes me.'"

Dave Spikey

"I knew I was going bald when it was taking longer and longer to wash my face."

Harry Hill

"I went to the dentist. He said, 'Say aaah.' I said, 'Why?' He said, 'My dog's died.'"

Tim Vine

A DIY enthusiast walks into his local library and asks: "Do you have any books on shelves?"

The girl behind the counter said: "They're all on shelves."

Tam Cowan, Daily Record

"Politician, woman, lobster, grass… That's it. No, wait! The sex of a fish. The big sex of a sports fish. Or maybe the little sex of a sports fish. A stickleback. You know what I'm saying?"

Eric Cantona, asked to describe himself in five words

David Beckham is celebrating. "Forty-three days, forty-three days!" he shouts happily. Posh asks him why he's celebrating.

He answers " I've done this jigsaw in only 43 days."

"And that's good?" asks Posh.

"You bet," says David. "It says three to six years on the box."

"I was doing a gig the other day and got talking to a girl in the front row. I asked her name and she said, 'it's Pataka'. I said that's a name you don't hear everyday. To which she replied, 'actually I do.'"

Jimmy Carr

"A cop pulled me over for running a stop sign. He said, 'Didn't you see the stop sign?' I said, 'Yeah, but I don't believe everything I read.'"

Steven Wright

"I love the way the Brits treat me – not like an airhead but as the businesswoman I am."

"Businesswoman" Paris Hilton threatens to move to Britain.

"He looks like a fish up a tree. Out of his depth."

Paul Merson's latest punditry gem

"The thing I've noticed about this World Cup is that it has a very international feel to it."

Perceptive punditry from Five Live*'s Jimmy Armfield*

"*Deal Or No Deal* might as well be called *Who Wants To Be A Millionaire For Thick People*. 'Do you know anything?' 'No!' 'Can you open a box?' 'Yes!' 'Alright!' Then Noel Edmonds starts pacing the floor like a creepy lizard wearing spray-on trousers. And he keeps saying things like, 'Oh, you're playing a very shrewd game here.' Shrewd? I'm pointing at a box!"

Russell Howard, Mock The Week

"No-one deserves to be booed. Well some people do. Like Myra Hindley or Anne Robinson"

Big Brother's Glyn equates serial child killer to the ginger gameshow hostess

The Manchester United players are in the dressing room before a game, when Roy Keane walks in. "Boss," he says, "there's a problem. I'm not playing unless I get a cortisone injection." "Hey," says Becks. "If he's having a new car, so am I."

"I'm so hot at the moment, I can turn anything on – animal, plant or mineral."

Modest mineral-brained Paris Hilton

"So I went down the local supermarket, I said 'I want to make a complaint, this vinegar's got lumps in it', he said 'Those are pickled onions.'"

Peter Kay

"Yeah, I had to do a karaoke song. No-one escapes that little initiation rite. I did "I'll Stand By You". I don't even know who sings it, I just went for an easy one."

Note to Ashley Cole: your wife's band Girls Aloud had a No 1 with that tune.

"My son Foster is a fan of the sport. He was a goaltender. His elder brother was a defenseman."

Liverpool's American owner George Gillett impresses Anfield with his soccerball knowledge

Q. How do you find a blind man in a nudist colony?
A. It's not hard.

A woman's husband has been slipping in and out of a coma for months, yet she's stayed by his bedside every single day.

One day, he awakes and whispers, "It's amazing. Though all my bad times, you've been with me. When I got fired, you were there. When I got shot, you were by my side. When I lost a leg in a car crash, you were there. When we lost the house, you stayed. When my health started failing, you were still by my side. You know what?'"

She says, "What, darling?"

He says, "You must be bad luck: piss off!"

Did you hear about the short-sighted circumciser?
He got the sack.

A bloke with a black eye boards a plane. He notices the bloke next to him has a black eye, too. He says, "Mind if I ask how you got yours?"

The other bloke says, "It was a tongue-twister accident. I was at the ticket counter and I got served by a blonde with huge breasts. Instead of saying, 'I'd like two tickets to Pittsburgh', I accidentally said, 'I'd like two pickets to Tittsburgh'. So she belted me."

The first bloke says, "Wow! mine was a tongue-twister too. I was at breakfast this morning and I wanted to say to my wife, 'Please pour me a bowl of Frosties, darling'. But I accidentally said, "You ruined my life, you evil slag."'

Q.   How does a man take a bubble bath?

A.   He eats baked beans for dinner.

Q.   What do a cheap hotel and a tight pair of pants have in common?

A.   No ballroom.

Q.   Why do men pay more than women for car insurance?

A.   Because women don't get blow-jobs while they're driving.

A boy born with no eyelids is to have pioneering surgery using foreskins. His parents are hoping it won't leave him cock-eyed.

A bloke walks into a psychiatrist's office wearing only clingfilm.

The shrink says, "I can clearly see you're nuts."

Q.   Why do men die before their wives?

A.   They want to.

Q.   What's the difference between men and women?

A.   A woman wants one man to satisfy her every need. A man wants every woman to satisfy his one need.

Q.   What's the difference between an egg and a wank?

A.   You can't beat a wank.

Three men on a road trip have to stay the night at a hotel and, short of money, end up sharing a bed.

In the morning the guy who'd slept on the left says, "Wow, I had a great dream last night. I was being given a hand-job by the most beautiful woman."

The man who'd slept on the right says, "That's strange; I had the exact same dream."

The man who'd slept in the middle says, "Well, I dreamed I was skiing."

After a night out, a bloke and his date are driving home in his car when they get pulled over by the police. The policeman says to the bloke, "Have you been drinking, sir?"

Surprised, the bloke says, "To be honest, yes. But I was driving carefully. How could you tell?"

"Your driving was fine," says the policeman. "It was the fat, ugly bird in the passenger seat that gave you away."

In the beginning, God created Earth and rested. Then God created man and rested. Then God created woman.

Since then, neither God nor man has rested.

Q. Why do men find it difficult to make eye contact?
A. Breasts don't have eyes.

Q. What's a man's idea of foreplay?
A. Half an hour of begging.

Q. How do you know when you're getting old?
A. When you start having dry dreams and wet farts.

Q. Why did God create men?
A. Because a vibrator can't mow the lawn.

God calls Adam and says, "I have some good news and some bad news. Which would you like to hear first?"

Adam says, "The good news."

God says, "I've given you a penis and a brain."

Adam says, "What's the bad news?"

God says, "I only gave you enough blood to operate one at a time."

A policeman comes to tell an Irish woman about her husband's untimely drowning in a vat of beer at the brewery.

She sobs, "Oh, the poor man. Please, tell me: did he suffer much?"

The policeman says, "I don't think so; he came out three times to piss."

Q. Who's the world's greatest athlete?
A. The bloke who finishes both first and third in a masturbation contest.

Q. What's the difference between hard and light?
A. You can go to sleep with a light on.

Q. Why is there a hole in a bloke's penis?
A. So he can get air to his brain.

Q. Why did the Irishman put ice in his condom?
A. To bring the swelling down.

Q. How do men sort their laundry?
A. 'Dirty' and 'Dirty but wearable'.

Q. What do you call the insensitive bit at the base of the penis?
A. The man.

A bloke comes running through the front door of his house screaming, "I've won the lottery! Pack your bags!"

His wife says, "Great! What shall I pack?"

He says, "I don't care; just get the fuck out of my house!"

A police officer finds a bloke in an alley with his finger up another man's arse.

"What are you doing?" asks the policeman.

"It's all right," says the bloke. "He's been drinking and I'm trying to make him sick."

"You won't make him sick by shoving your finger up his arse," says the policeman.

The bloke says, "I will when I put it in his mouth."

Q. What do you call 12 naked men sitting on each other's shoulders?

A. A scrotum pole.

A bloke moves into a new flat, and goes to the lobby to put his name on the group letterbox.

While he's there, an attractive young woman comes out of the flat next to the letterboxes, wearing only a dressing-gown.

The bloke smiles at the woman and she strikes up a conversation with him. As they talk, her dressing-gown slips open, and it's obvious she's got nothing on underneath.

The poor bloke breaks into a sweat trying to maintain eye contact.

After a few minutes, the woman places her hand on his arm and says, "Let's go in my flat; I hear someone coming…"

He follows her into the flat, and after she closes the door, she leans against it, allowing her dressing-gown to fall off completely.

Completely naked, she purrs, "What would you say is the best part of my body?"

Blushing, the bloke says, "It's got to be your ears."

Astounded, the woman says, "My ears? Look at my breasts! They're big, don't sag, and they're completely natural. My bum is firm and has no cellulite on it. Look at my skin – no spots or scars. Why the hell would you say my ears are the best part of my body?"

The bloke says, "You know outside when you said you heard someone coming? That was me."

Two old friends meet for the first time in 40 years.
The first says, "Bill, you look like you did 40 years ago. What's your secret?"

Bill replies, "Plastic surgery. It's really great, but now my belly-button is at the back of my head."

His friend looks disgusted.

Bill says, "If you think that's weird, you should see what I'm wearing as a tie."

Three men are travelling and looking for a place to stay. Eventually they come across a convent and ask the Mother Superior if they can stay the night.

She says, "If I catch you looking at my nuns in the showers, I'll have to cut your dicks off."

Sure enough, they get caught, and she asks the first man, "What's your job?"

"A butcher."

"Then I'll cut your dick off with a knife."

The second guy says he's a joiner, so the nun says, "I'll cut yours off with a saw."

Finally she turns to the third man and says the same, to which he replies, "I'm a lollipop man. What are you gonna do – suck it?"

A man puts his father in a nursing home.

The old man cries, "Please don't put me in there, son."

The son says, "Dad, I can't take care of you. I've checked the place out and it's the best there is. I think you'll love it."

The next day the old man calls his son and says, "Son, you were right! I love this place."

The son says, "Glad to hear it. What makes it so great?"

The old man says, "Last night I was in my room and from out of nowhere, I got an erection. A nurse came in, saw my hard-on and gave me a blow-job! I haven't had one of those in 30 years! I'd almost forgotten what it was like! It was fantastic!"

A few days later, the old man calls his son again and says, "You have to get me out of here. I hate this place."

The son says, "What's wrong?"

The old man says, "Last night I fell down in the corridor. While I was still on my hands and knees, a male nurse came along and took me up the arse. I can't go on like this."

The son says, "Dad, I know that's terrible and we'll get it sorted out, but until then, you have to take the rough with the smooth."

The old man says, "No, you don't understand. I get an erection maybe once a year, but I fall down two or three times a day."

A bloke goes into a jeweller's, unzips his flies and pulls out his penis. Unfazed, the saleswoman says, "This is a clock shop, not a cock shop."

The bloke says, "OK, put two hands on it."

Q. What's the difference between a peeping tom and a thief?

A. A thief snatches watches.

John goes to the doctors and says, "Doctor, you've got to help me – I just can't get a hard-on."

So the doctor examines his cock and says, "Your cock muscles are too weak. We're going to have to take the muscles from an elephant's cock and graft them on to your penis."

John's desperate for sex, so he agrees.

After the op, John goes out on a dinner date with a new girl. But half-way through the meal, his cock starts to feel strange and uncomfortably big, so to release the strain he unzips his flies under the table.

Suddenly his cock springs out of his trousers, grabs a bun from the next table and shoots back into his trousers with it.

His date is stunned and says, "Christ, you've got a huge cock. Can you do that again?"

John replies, "Well, I could try, but I don't think I can fit another bun up my arse."

Jeff walks into a pub and sees his friend Paul slumped miserably at the bar. He goes over to ask what's wrong.

"Well," says Paul. "You know that beautiful girl at work who I wanted to ask out, but couldn't because I got an embarrassing erection every time I saw her?"

"Yes," says Jeff.

"I finally plucked up the courage to ask her out, and she agreed."

"That's great," says Jeff. "When are you going out?"

"I went to meet her this evening," says Paul, "but I was worried I'd get an erection again. So I got some duct tape and taped my penis to my leg, so that if I did get a hard-on, it wouldn't show."

"Good thinking," says Jeff.

"So I get to her door," says Paul, "and I rang the doorbell. She answered it in the tiniest dress you ever saw."

"And what happened then?"

"I kicked her in the face."

Q. Why are blokes like public toilets?
A. They're either vacant, engaged or full of crap.

Q. What does a Scotsman wear under his kilt?
A. Lipstick, on a good day.

Two married blokes are out drinking one night when one says, "I don't know what else to do. Whenever I go home after we've been out drinking, I turn the headlights off before I get to the driveway. I shut off the engine and coast into the garage. I take my shoes off before I go into the house. I sneak up the stairs. I get undressed in the bathroom. I ease into bed… and my wife still wakes up and yells, 'and what time do you call this?'"

His mate looks at him and says, "Well, you're obviously taking the wrong approach. I screech into the driveway, slam the door, clatter up the steps, chuck my shoes against the wall, jump into bed, slap my wife's arse and say, 'How about a blow-job?' And she's always sound asleep."

Q. Why do men take showers instead of baths?
A. Pissing in the bath is disgusting.

Q. Why do men have a spine?
A. If they didn't, they'd suck their cocks all day long.

Two IT guys are walking through the park when one says, "Where did you get such a great bike?"

The second IT guy says, "I was walking along yesterday, minding my own business, when a beautiful woman rode up on this bike. She threw the bike to the ground, took off all her clothes and said, 'Take what you want.'"

The second IT guy nods approvingly and says, "Good choice – the clothes probably wouldn't have fitted."

One day, at the dinner table, a son asks his father, "Dad, how many kinds of breasts are there?"

The father says, "Son, there are three types. In her twenties, a woman's breasts are like melons, round and firm. In her thirties to forties, they're like pears, still nice but drooping a bit. After 50, they're like onions."

"Onions?" says the son.

"Yes, you see them and they make you cry."

This infuriates his mum and daughter, so the daughter

says, "Mum, how many kinds of penises are there?"

The mother looks at her husband and says, "Well, dear, a man goes through three phases. In his twenties, his penis is like an oak, mighty and hard. In his thirties to forties, it's like a birch, flexible but reliable. After his fifties, it's like a Christmas tree."

"A Christmas tree?" says the daughter.

"Yes, dead from the root up and the balls are for decoration only."

At the end of the tax year, the Tax Office sends an inspector to audit the books of a synagogue.

While he's checking the books, he says to the Rabbi, "I notice you buy a lot of candles. What do you do with the candle drippings?"

The Rabbi says, "We save them up and send them back to the candle-makers, and every now and then they send us a complete box of candles."

The tax inspector says, "What about all these matzo balls you buy? What do you do with the crumbs?"

The Rabbi says, "We collect them and send them back to the manufacturers, and every now and then they send a complete box of matzo balls."

The tax inspector says, "And what do you do with all the leftover foreskins from the circumcisions you perform?"

The Rabbi says, "Here, too, we do not waste. We save up all the foreskins and send them to the Tax Office, and about once a year they send us a complete dick."

Three old men are complaining about how much their hands shake.

The first old bloke says, "My hands shake so bad that when I shaved this morning, I cut my face."

The second old bloke says, "Oh, yeah? Well, my hands shake so bad that when I trimmed my garden yesterday, I sliced all my flowers."

The third old bloke says, "That's nothing. My hands shake so bad that when I took a piss yesterday, I came three times."

Q. What did the left testicle say to the right testicle?
A. Dunno, but they were talking bollocks.

Q. What do toy train sets and breasts have in common?
A. They're usually intended for children, but it's the men who end up playing with them.

GIRLS

What's the difference between a woman on her period and a terrorist?

You can negotiate with a terrorist.

"I've got no problem buying tampons. I'm a modern man. But apparently, they're not a 'proper' present."

Jimmy Carr

What do you call a room full of women, half with PMS, half with yeast infections?
A whine and cheese party

"I met a Dutch girl with inflatable shoes last week, phoned her up to arrange a date but unfortunately she'd popped her clogs."

Peter Kay

A blonde with two burnt ears goes to the doctor, who asks what has happened. "The phone rang, and I accidentally picked up the iron."

"What about the other one?"

"They called back."

A man approached a very beautiful woman in a large supermarket and asked, "You know, I've lost my wife here in the supermarket. Can you talk to me for a couple of minutes?"

"Why?"

"Because every time I talk to a beautiful woman my wife appears out of nowhere."

Q. What is the similarity between PlayStations and breasts?

A. Both are made for children, but used by adults.

What's the difference between BSE and PMT?
One is mad cow disease while the other has something to do with beef.

A man is speeding down a narrow mountain road, when a woman comes hurtling round the corner. He swerves to avoid her, but as she passes she leans out the window and screams "PIG!"

Astonished, the man turns and yells back, "BITCH!" as he reaches the bend and crashes into a pig.

Why are hurricanes named after women?

Because when they come, they're wild and wet, and when they go they take your house and car with them.

How can you tell if your wife is dead? The sex is the same but the dishes pile up.

Three women went out drinking, and decided to have a contest of who could get the drunkest. The next day the women all got together. The first woman said, "I drove my car into a ditch."

The second woman said, "I blew chunks."

The third woman said, "I burned down my house."

After they all had told their stories, the third woman said, "I guess I won."

The second woman replied, "You don't understand, Chunks is my dog."

What do a woman and Kentucky Fried Chicken have in common?
By the time you've finished on the breast and thighs, all you have left is a greasy box for the bone.

The last fight we had was my fault. My wife asked, "What's on the TV?"

I said, "Dust."

How do you give a woman more freedom?
Make the kitchen larger.

Q. Why are bachelors thin, and married men fat?
A. Bachelors come home, check to see what's in the fridge, and go to bed. Married men come home, check to see what's in the bed, and go the fridge.

Doctors have found that single women can't fart. They don't have an arsehole until they get married.

"The other day I sent my girlfriend a huge pile of snow. I rang her up, I said 'Did you get my drift?'"

Peter Kay

If your dog's barking at the back door and your wife's knocking at the front door whom would you let in first?
The dog, because he'll shut up once he's in.

A beautiful, voluptuous woman goes to see a gynaecologist. Right away he tells her to undress. After she has disrobed he strokes her thigh.

As he does, he says to the woman: "Do you know what I'm doing?"

"Yes," she says, "you're checking for any abrasions or dermatological abnormalities."

"Correct," says the doctor.

He then fondles her breasts. "Do you know what I'm doing now", he says.

"Yes," says the woman, "you're checking for any lumps or breast cancer."

"That's right," replies the doctor. He then proceeds to have sex with her. "Do you know," he pants, "what I'm doing now?"

"Yes," she says. "You're getting herpes."

What does a woman of 40 have between her breasts that a woman of 20 doesn't?

A belly-button.

What's the white stuff you find in the bottom of girls' undies?
  Clitty litter.

Q. How do you annoy your girlfriend during sex?
A. Phone her.

A taxi pulls up outside a lady's house. The cabbie turns around and says: "That'll be £12."
  The woman in the back has no money, so instead she pulls up her skirt and spreads her legs. "Can I pay with this?" she asks.
  "Christ!" the cabbie replies. "Haven't you got anything smaller?"

A study in the UK showed that the kind of male face a woman finds attractive can differ on where a woman is in her menstrual cycle. For instance, if she is ovulating, she is attracted to men with rugged, masculine features.
  And if she's menstruating she's more prone to be attracted to a man with scissors shoved in his temple.

A banana and a vibrator are sitting on a woman's bedside table. The banana says, "I don't know why you're shaking; she's going to bloody eat me."

A blonde walks into a chemist's and asks the assistant for some anal deodorant.

The chemist, a little bemused, explains to the woman that they don't sell anal deodorant, and never have done.

Unfazed, the blonde assures the chemist she's often bought the stuff from this shop and would like some more.

"I'm sorry," says the chemist. "Do you have the container it came in?"

"Yes," says the blonde, producing it from her handbag.

The chemist says, "But this is just a normal stick of under-arm deodorant."

The blonde replies, "But the label says, 'To apply, push up bottom.'"

Scientists have discovered that beer contains female hormones. In tests, they gave three men 12 pints each – they all talked crap, gained weight and couldn't drive.

A blonde visits her gynaecologist.

He peers between her legs. "Christ, you've got a big vagina… Christ, you've got a big vagina."

She says, "You don't need to say it twice."

He says, "I didn't."

Q. What's the difference between a blonde and a stationery cupboard?

A. You can only fit two men at once in a stationery cupboard.

Q. Why did the blonde stop using the Pill?

A. Because it kept falling out.

A blonde walks into a shop and asks the bloke behind the counter if she can buy a picture frame.

The bloke says, "Do you wanna screw for it?"

The blonde says, "No, but I'll give you a blow-job for that lampshade."

Q. How can you tell if a blonde's used your computer?

A. The joystick's wet.

A bloke picks up a young blonde and takes her back to his hotel room.

After they have sex, he says, "Am I the first man you've had sex with?"

She says, "You might be; your face looks familiar."

Q. What's the difference between a blonde and an ironing board?

A. An ironing board's legs are difficult to part.

A blonde pushes her BMW into a petrol station.

She tells the mechanic the engine's died. After he's worked on it for a few minutes, it's running smoothly again.

She says, "What's the story?"

He replies, "Just crap in the carburettor.'"

She says, 'OK, how often do I have to do that?'

Q. What's the difference between a blonde and the
    Titanic?
A. Only 1,500 went down on the *Titanic*.

Q. Why is a blonde like a railway track?
A. Because she's been laid all over the country.

Q. Why is a blonde like an old washing machine?
A. They both drip when they're fucked.

A blonde is involved in a serious car crash. The paramedics
arrive and drag her out of the car, lying her flat on the
ground.

    The first paramedic says, "I'm going to check if you're
concussed. How many fingers am I putting up?"

    The blonde says, "Oh, my God – I'm paralysed from the
waist down!"

**A blonde walks into the dry cleaners.
She places a garment on the counter
and says, "I'll be back tomorrow
afternoon to pick up my dress."**

**"Come again?" says the deaf old
assistant, cupping his ear.**

**"No," she says, "this time it's
mayonnaise."**

Q. What do blondes put behind their ears to attract
    blokes?
A. Their knees.

A blonde goes to the council to register for child benefit.
"How many children?" asks the council worker.

"Ten," says the blonde.

"Ten?" says the council worker. "What are their names?"

"Wayne, Wayne, Wayne, Wayne, Wayne, Wayne, Wayne, Wayne, Wayne and Wayne."

"Doesn't that get confusing?"

"No," says the blonde. "It's great, because if they're out playing in the street I just have to shout, 'Wayne, your dinner's ready' or, 'Wayne, go to bed now', and they all do it."

"But what if you want to speak to one individually?" asks the council worker.

"Easy," says the blonde. "I just use their surnames."

A bloke comes home to find his girlfriend having sex with his best mate.

He says, "What's going on here?"

The girlfriend turns to the mate and says, "You See? I told you he was stupid."

Two blondes meet up.

The first one says, "My boyfriend bought me a bunch of flowers on Friday evening. I had to keep my legs open all weekend."

The other says, "Why? Didn't you have a vase?"

Q. Why do blondes wear knickers?
A. To keep their ankles warm.

A blonde and an Irishman are in a pub when the blonde notices something strange about the wellies the Irishman is wearing.

She says, "Why does one of your wellies have an L written on it, while the other has an R?"

The Irishman says, "It helps me remember. The one with the L is my left boot and the one with the R is my right."

"Ah," says the blonde, "so that's why my knickers have got C&A on them."

Q.   How does a blonde turn on the light after sex?
A.   She opens the car door.

Q.   What nursery rhyme do blondes learn as kids?
A.   Hump Me Dump Me.

A blonde says to her therapist, "Kiss me, kiss me!"
The therapist says, "No, that's unethical. I shouldn't even be shagging you."

Q.   Why did the blonde have rectangular breasts?
A.   She forgot to take the tissues out of the box.

Q.   What does a blonde say after multiple orgasms?
A.   "Thanks, team!"

Q.   What's the best thing about a blow-job?
A.   Five minutes of silence.

Q. What do bottle-blondes and airliners have in common?

A. They both have black boxes.

A blonde enters a sex shop and asks for a vibrator.

The assistant says, "Choose from our range on the wall."

She says, "I'll take the big red one."

The assistant says, "That's a fire extinguisher."

A bloke arrives home to find his wife in front of a mirror stretching her arms, chanting, "I must, I must improve my bust."

The bloke says, "What are you doing?"

His wife says, "An exercise to make my boobs bigger."

The bloke says, "That doesn't work. What you need to do is rub toilet paper between them."

His wife says, "And that will make them bigger?"

The bloke says, "Well, it worked on your arse."

Two gynaecologists meet up.

One says, "I had a patient today with breasts like melons."

The other says, "Wow, that big?"

"Yes, that big."

"Well, I had a patient with a clitoris like a lemon."

"Wow, that big?"

"No, that sour."

Q. How do you make a blonde burn her face?
A. Ring her when she's doing the ironing.

Q. Why do women like circumcised cocks?
A. They can't resist anything with 10 per cent off.

Did you hear about the woman with no arms and no legs who won the strawberry-picking competition? Jammy twat!

A man doesn't like his daughter's boyfriend and decides to confront her.

"That boyfriend of yours isn't good enough for you," he says. "He's the stupidest bloke I've ever met."

"Daddy," she replies, "he's not stupid. We've only been together nine weeks and already he's cured that little illness I used to have every month."

Q. Who helped God design woman?
A. The council – who else would put a playground next to a shithole?

Q. Why is the book *Women Who Love Too Much* a disappointment for male readers?
A. No phone numbers.

Q. Why do men fart more often than women?
A. Because women can't shut up long enough to build up the required pressure.

A fat woman says to her gynaecologist, "I don't enjoy sex any more."

The gynaecologist says, "Why don't you diet?"

The woman says, "OK, then – what colour?"

Q. How do you piss off a female archaeologist?
A. Show her a used tampon and ask her which period it came from.

Q. What makes five pounds of fat look really good?
A. A nipple.

Q. How do you turn a fox into a Rottweiler?
A. Marry her.

Q. What's the difference between a girlfriend and a wife?
A. About two stone.

It's my girlfriend's birthday soon, so I bought her a handbag and a dildo.
If she doesn't like the handbag, she can go fuck herself.

Little Annie wanders into the bathroom while her dad is in the bath.

She looks down at his tackle and says, "What's that, Daddy?"

Her dad looks sheepish and replies, "Er… it's my hedgehog, darling."

Little Annie says, "Christ, it's got a big dick."

What woman can wash up with her left hand, dry up with her right, mop with one leg and dust with the other, while giving a blow-job and opening you a beer with her arse? A Swiss army wife.

Two women walking home drunk need to pee, so they duck into a graveyard.

They don't have any toilet paper, so the first woman uses her knickers, then throws them away. The other finds a ribbon from a wreath and uses that.

The next day their husbands are talking. The first says, "We'd better keep an eye on our wives. Mine came home last night with no knickers on."

The second says, "You think that's bad? Mine had a card stuck on her arse that said, 'From all the lads at the fire station; we'll never forget you.'"

"Everything looks neat and tidy in there," says the gynaecologist to the lesbian.

"So it should be," says the lesbian. "I have a woman in twice a week."

A little girl goes to the barber with her father.

She stands next to the barber's chair, eating a cake while her dad gets his hair cut.

The barber smiles at her and says, "Sweetheart, you're going to get hair on your muffin."

"I know," she says. "I'm gonna get tits, too."

Q. How can you tell you have a high sperm count?
A. Your girlfriend has to chew before she swallows.

Q. What do you call a lesbian dinosaur?
A. A lickalotapuss.

Nike have developed a new pair of trainers for lesbians called Nikes For Dykes. They come with an extra-long tongue and you can get them off with one finger.

Q. How do you spot a macho woman?
A. She's rolling her own tampons.

Q. How do you define "making love"?
A. Something a woman does while a bloke is shagging her.

Two nuns are decorating the vestry and to save getting paint on their habits, they decide to do it in the nude. Suddenly there's a knock at the door.

"Who is it?" asks Sister Mary, looking shocked.

"It's the blind man," comes the reply from behind the door.

"Oh, that's OK," says Sister Angelica, "let him in."

Sister Mary opens the door and as the bloke enters he says, "Nice tits, love – now, where do you want these blinds?"

Q. What are the small bumps around a woman's nipples?
A. It's Braille for "Suck here".

One bloke says to another, "I haven't spoken to my wife for 18 months."

The other bloke says, "Why not?"

The first bloke says, "I don't like to interrupt her."

What's it called when a woman is paralysed from the waist down?

Marriage.

Q. Why do women call period pains PMS?

A. Mad Cow Disease was already taken.

Two old women are having coffee when one asks the other, "Did you come on the bus?"

The other one says, "Yes, but I managed to make it look like an asthma attack."

A lady walks into a shop which sells Persian rugs. She spots the perfect rug and walks over to inspect it. As she bends over to feel its texture, she farts loudly. Embarrassed, she looks around to see if anyone has noticed. Standing nearby is a salesman.

He says, "Good day, madam. How may we help you?"

Uncomfortably, she says, "What's the price of this rug?"

He says, "Madam, if you farted just touching it, you'll shit yourself when you hear the price."

Q. Why did God give men penises?

A. So they'd have a way to stop a woman talking.

Bruce is driving over the Sydney Harbour Bridge one day when he sees his girlfriend about to throw herself off.

Bruce slams on the brakes and yells, "Sheila, what the hell are you doing?"

Sheila turns round with a tear in her eye and says, "G'day, Bruce. You got me pregnant and so now I'm gonna kill myself."

Bruce gets a lump in his throat when he hears this and says, "Strewth, Sheila – not only are you a great shag, you're a real sport, too."

Q.   What's the difference between a drug dealer and a prostitute?
A.   A prostitute can wash her crack and sell it again.

Q.   Why do women rub their eyes when they wake up?
A.   Because they don't have bollocks to scratch.

A blonde is waiting for a bus when a strong gust of wind lifts her skirt and reveals she isn't wearing any knickers.

A nearby bloke, wanting to put her at ease, jokes, "Airy, isn't it?"

"Well, what did you expect?" she replies. "Feathers?"

Q.   Why does the bride always smile on her wedding day?
A.   Because she knows she's given her last blow-job.

Q. What do you call a woman who can suck a golf ball through a hose?
A. "Darling."

Q. What do you call a tattooed prostitute?
A. A scenic root.

Q. What do tornadoes and marriage have in common?
A. They both start with a lot of blowing and in the end you lose your house.

A woman has a new job collecting the sperm from turkeys to use for artificial insemination.

On the first day, as she approaches one turkey, it goes: "Gobble gobble."

She says, "Quiet! You'll settle for a hand-job like the rest!"

Q. What's the difference between your wife and your job?
A. After 10 years your job still sucks.

Two lesbians are walking down the street with their hands down each other's knickers.

A man walks by and says, "Why are you doing that?"

The first lesbian says, "We're lip-reading."

Q. What's the difference between a whore and a bitch?
A. A whore sleeps with everyone at a party and a bitch sleeps with everyone but you.

Q. What's the difference between a woman from Wigan and a walrus?
A. One's got a moustache and smells of fish and the other lives in the sea.

One bloke asks another, "Have you ever gone to bed with an ugly woman?"
The second bloke says, "No, but I've woken up with plenty."

A husband and wife are getting ready for bed.

The wife is standing in front of a full-length mirror taking a long hard look at herself.

"You know, dear," she says, "I look in the mirror and I see an old woman. My face is wrinkled, my boobs barely clear my waist and my arse is sagging. I've got fat legs and my arms are flabby. Tell me something positive to make me feel better about myself."

He says, "Well, there's nothing wrong with your eyesight."

Q. What do your wife and a vacuum cleaner have in common?
A. After a year they stop sucking and start whining.

A couple go to bed for the first time.

The woman says, "Oh, dear, what a small organ."

The bloke says, "Well, I didn't think I'd be playing in the town hall."

A bloke walks into a lift and stands next to a beautiful woman.

After a few seconds he turns to her and says, "Can I smell your knickers?"

The woman says, "Certainly not!"

The man says, "Hmm. It must be your feet, then."

A woman visits her doctor to complain about strange abdominal pains.

He examines her and says, "I hope you're looking forward to many sleepless nights because of crying and nappy-changing."

"Why," says the woman, "am I pregnant?"

"No," says the doctor, "you've got bowel cancer."

A woman goes to her doctor to complain about the side-effects of the testosterone pills he'd given her.

She says, "Doctor, I'm wondering if you got the dosage right. I've started growing hair in places I've never grown hair before."

The doctor says, "A little growth is a perfectly normal side-effect of testosterone. Just where has this happened?"

She says, "On my balls."

A woman in her late forties goes to a plastic surgeon for a face-lift.

The surgeon tells her about a new procedure called The Knob, in which a small knob is placed on the top of a woman's head and can be turned to tighten her skin, producing the effect of a face-lift.

She has the op. Over the next few years, she regularly tightens her knob and stays youthful and pretty.

However, after 15 years she returns to the surgeon with two problems. She says, "First, I have these terrible bags under my eyes and The Knob won't get rid of them."

The doctor says, "Those aren't bags; those are your breasts."

She says, "Well, I suppose there's no point asking about the goatee."

During sex, a bloke says to his wife, "How come you never tell me when you have an orgasm?"
She says, "You're never home."

Two blokes are in a pub.

One says to the other, "I shagged your mum."

The other doesn't reply.

Again the first one shouts, "I shagged your mum."

The whole pub turns round to watch.

The other bloke says, "Go home, Dad, you're drunk."

Q. Why is the space between a woman's breasts and hips called a waist?

A. Because you could fit another pair of tits there.

Q. Why was alcohol invented?

A. So ugly women could get laid.

A woman goes to her boyfriend's parents' house for dinner. This is her first time meeting the family and she's very nervous.

They all sit down and start to eat. The woman is beginning to feel a little discomfort, thanks to the broccoli casserole. The build-up of wind makes her eyes water. Left with no choice, she lets out a dainty little fart.

Hearing it, her boyfriend's father looks over at the family dog snoozing at the woman's feet and sternly says, "Ginger!"

The woman smiles in relief.

A couple of minutes later, she feels the pain again. This time, she doesn't hesitate, and lets rip a much louder and longer fart.

The father again looks at the dog and yells, "Damn it, Ginger!"

Again the woman smiles in relief.

A few minutes later, the woman has to fart once more. This time she doesn't even think about it, and lets rip with a fart that would rival a foghorn.

The father looks at the dog in disgust and yells, "Damn it, Ginger, get away from her before she shits on you!"

Q. What do women and clouds have in common?
A. Eventually they piss off and it's a nice day.

Two women are playing golf.
After hitting par on the first hole, they make their way to the second. Suddenly they hear a cry of "Fore!" and one of the women gets hit on the head by a ball and collapses.
The second woman runs back to the clubhouse to get help.
She cries, "My friend has been hit with a ball. Can someone come and look?"
The nearest bloke says, "Sure, where was she hit?"
"Between the first and second holes."
"Well, that doesn't leave much room for a plaster."

Q. What do women and cow pats have in common?
A. The older they get, the easier they are to pick up.

Q. Why are women like orange juice cartons?
A. It's not the size or shape that matters, or even how sweet the juice inside is: it's getting the bloody flaps open.

Q. Why are women like pianos?
A. When they're not upright, they're grand.

Q. Why are women like parking spaces?
A. All the good ones are taken and the ones left are handicapped.

Q. What's the difference between a woman and a washing machine?
A. A washing machine doesn't expect you to ring after you've dumped your load in it.

Q. Why do only ten per cent of women go to heaven?
A. Because if they all went, it would be hell.

Q. Why did God let women have orgasms?
A. It gives them another reason to moan.

Q. Why do they call it the Wonderbra?
A. Because when she takes it off, you wonder where her tits went.

Q. What is a zebra?
A. Twenty-five sizes larger than an 'A' bra.

GOING HOLLYWOOD

"I hope all my new work will help producers get past my hotness."

Jessica Alba: immodest but factually accurate

"I once tried to chat up Kate Winslet. She either didn't hear me or she ignored me."

Will Ferrell shrugs off a ginger blow-out

"I love to put on lotion. Sometimes I'll watch TV and go into a lotion trance for an hour, just rubbing it in"

Angelina Jolie. We're in a trance just thinking about it

"Fuck this. I'll buy the fucking hotel"

Hollywood big nob Harvey Weinstein, after being told that a Caribbean private beach was for hotel residents only

"I'm afraid sir, the fucking hotel isn't for sale. Good day."

Hotel manager's ice cool reply

"There's nothing worse than a sex scene where someone's got a T-shirt on or a strategic sheet over them. It's unrealistic. If you're going to do it, do it."

Sienna Miller vows to give us something to look at

"She gets her boobs out all the time and it's considered art."

Jordan gets jealous of Sienna Miller

"I'll pick out two outfits, one which is disgusting and one nice and I'll ask my 'friend' what they think. If they go for the revolting one, I cut them out of my life."

Paris Hilton on how she weeds out her friends

"People love me in my underwear. It's a public service. If I'm not in my underwear by page 50 of the script, I'm not happy"

Will Ferrell embraces semi-nude scenes

"Sex scenes are easy. I don't have a problem with them. Actually it was quite liberating to be out in the desert, completely topless, with a beautiful Venezuelan guy."

Kiera Knightley recalls rude scenes in Domino.
Men worldwide curse the "beautiful Venezuelan" bit

"If I were a guy, I'd ask Cameron to marry me. She has the cutest, tightest butt and she's also a world-class belcher."

Eva Mendes on Cameron Diaz, and who are we to argue?

"I read the book, read the script, saw the film and still don't understand it."

Sean Connery on why he turned down the role of Gandalf in Lord Of The Rings.

"I love filming sex scenes with women"

Angelina Jolie's claim is music to our ears

"She has the naughtiest eyes in showbusiness. When she looks you straight in the eye, it's stunning."

Daniel Craig has a crush on his Bond boss Dame Judie Dench

"I got gashed above my right eye but just rubbed a little dirt on it and kept going. Chicks dig scars."

Bruce Willis after getting kicked in the forehead filming a fight scenes

READERS

Why do elephants drink? To forget.

Two antennas met on a roof, fell in love and got married. The ceremony wasn't much, but the reception was excellent.

Two peanuts walk into a bar and one was a salted.

Before bed one night, Arsene Wenger is trying to think of ways to get Arsenal's season back on track. As a last effort, he prays to God for guidance. God hears the Frenchman's whining and decides to take pity. Later that night Wenger suddenly awakes to see The Lord standing at the bottom of his bed. "Come forth my son!" says God. To which Wenger replies, "Fourth? We'll be lucky if we finish bloody sixth!"

Q. How does Michael Jackson pick his nose?
A. From a catalogue.

A man wakes up and says to his wife, "I had a wet dream about you last night!" "Aww, did you?" she says. "Yeah, I dreamt you were hit by a bus and I pissed myself laughing!"

One day a guy dies and finds himself in hell. As he is wallowing in despair, he has his first meeting with the devil…

Satan: "Why so glum?"

Guy: "What do you think? I'm in hell!"

Satan: "Hell's not so bad. We actually have a lot of fun down here. You a drinking man?"

Guy: "Sure, I love to drink."

Satan: "Well, you're gonna love Mondays then. On Mondays, that's all we do is drink. Whiskey, tequila, Guinness, wine coolers, Tab, and Fresca. We drink 'til we throw up, and then we drink some more! And you don't have to worry about getting a hangover, because you're dead anyway."

Guy: "Gee that sounds great!"

Satan: "You a smoker?"

Guy: "You better believe it"

Satan: "All right! You're gonna love Tuesdays We get the finest cigars from all over the world, and smoke our lungs out. If you get cancer – no biggie, you're already dead, remember?"

Guy: "Wow… that's awesome!"

Satan: "I bet you like to gamble."

Guy: "Why, yes, as a matter of fact I do."

Satan: "Good, 'cause Wednesdays you can gamble all you want. Craps, blackjack, roulette, poker, slots, whatever. If you go bankrupt, it doesn't matter, you're dead anyhow."

Guy: "Cool!"

Satan: "What about Drugs?"

Guy: "Are you kidding? Love drugs! You don't mean…?"

Satan: "That's right! Thursday is drug day. Help yourself to a great big bowl of crack or smack. Smoke a joint the size of a submarine. You can do all the drugs you want. You're dead so who cares."

Guy: "Wow! I never realized Hell was such a cool place!"

Satan: "You gay?"

Guy: "No…"

Satan: "Ooooh, Fridays might be tough…"

Britain has won a gold medal in the Olympic's white water rafting event. Two blokes from Cornwall won it in a white transit van.

What do you call a bloke with three eyes?

Seymour.

What do you call a Spaniard who's had his motor nicked?

Carlos.

What's yellow and smells of bananas? Monkey sick.

What do Viagra and Alton Towers have in common?

They both make you to stand around for an hour waiting for a two-minute ride.

A Glastonbury Portaloo goes up to the bar and orders a pint of cider.

Barman says, 'No way, you're steaming.'

An old American guy was very ill and his son went to visit him in the hospital. He was sat on the bed, giving the old man some emotional words, when suddenly, the father began to breathe heavily. He grabbed a pen and pad from his bedside table. With his last ounce of strength, he scribbled a note, dropped it and died.

The son was so overcome with grief that he didn't remember slipping the note into his pocket. At the funeral, he reached into his coat and immediately felt the note. He excitedly read it thinking it might be something he could recite during the service. It read: "You thick wanker – get off my fucking oxygen pipe."

What's black and white, then black and brown, then black and black?

A nun roasting on a spit.

A bloke says to his wife "Why don't you tell me when you orgasm?" She replies, "I don't like ringing you at work."

A feminist visited Kuwait several years before the Gulf War and noted that women customarily walked about 10 feet behind their husbands. She returned to Kuwait recently and was surpised to see that the men now walked several yards behind their wives. Approaching one of the women for an explanation, she said: "This is marvellous. What enabled women here to achieve this reversal of gender roles?"

"Land mines," came the reply.

A driver is stopped for speeding. When asked for his occupation he replies "Rectum stretcher". What the fuck's that? asks the cop. The driver says you put 1 finger in, then 2, then a hand etc. until its 6ft wide. The cop asks, "What the fuck do you do with a 6ft arsehole?" The driver replies, "give it a uniform and a fucking speed gun."

A man says to his wife, "Put your coat on – I'm going to the pub." His wife says, "Ooh, lovely – are you taking me for a drink?" The man says, "No, I'm turning the heating off."

What's worse than having termites in your piano?
  Crabs on your organ.

One night, a man rolls over in bed and gives his wife a big, knowing grin. Immediately realising his intentions she says, "Not tonight darling. I have an appointment with the gynaecologist tomorrow morning and I want to stay fresh and clean."
  Disappointed, the husband rolls over and tries to get to sleep. A few minutes later, he rolls over and prods his wife again. "Tell me, do you have a dentist appointment tomorrow, too?"

Why do Buddhists refuse novocaine during root canal work?
  Because they want to transcend dental medication.

Why do brides dress in white?

So they match the rest of the appliances.

Two blokes are in a barber's shop. They've both just finished having a shave, and the barber reaches for some aftershave. The first bloke yells, "Hey! Don't put that cheap crap on me! My wife will think I've been in a brothel!" The second bloke turns to the barber and says, "Put it on me. My wife doesn't know what the inside of a brothel smells like."

A man presented his girlfriend with three choices of condom – gold, silver or bronze.

"Silver," she said.

"Why not gold?"

"Because I want you to come second for once."

A man goes to confession and says, "Father, I have been with a loose woman."

"Who was the woman?" The priest asks.

"I can't tell, Father. I don't want to ruin her reputation," the man replies.

The priest says, "I'm sure to find out, so you may as well say. Was it Brenda O'Malley?" The man won't tell. "Was it Patricia Kelly?" The man won't tell. "Was it Liz Shannon?" The man won't tell. "Was it Cathy Morgan?" The man won't tell. "Was it Fiona McDonald?" The man won't tell. The priest sighs and says, "You're steadfast, and I admire that. But you've sinned and must atone. You cannot attend church for three months. Be off with you."

The man walks back to his pew. His mate slides over and whispers, "What did you get?"

The man says, "Three months' vacation and five good leads."

A man goes to his GP and says, "Doc please help me! I've got a problem." The doctor examines him and finds a red ring around his penis. He gives him an ointment to rub on the problem area and tells him to come back the next day.

"It's all cleared up!" the man reports when he returns. "But what was that medication you gave me?"

"Lipstick remover," comes the reply.

After all the revelations about him in the press, David Hasselhoff has said he only wants to be known as The Hoff. I guess he just doesn't want the hassel any more.

Two blokes are talking. First bloke says, "I tried to kill myself yesterday by taking 1,000 aspirins.

"Second bloke says, "What happened?"

First bloke says, "Well, after the first two I felt better."

What's white and can't climb trees?

A fridge.

What's small, furry and hates sex?

The injured badger in the boot of my car.

A Catholic, a Baptist and a Mormon are bragging about the size of their families.

The Catholic says, "I have four boys and my wife is pregnant. One more son and I'll have a basketball team."

The Baptist says, "I can beat that. I have 10 boys, and my wife is pregnant. One more son and I'll have a football team."

The Mormon says, "That's nothing. I have 17 wives. One more and I'll have a golf course."

What's the difference between Sir Alex Ferguson and James Brown? Fergie will be playing Giggs this year.

A student visits a Bangkok massage parlour. A sexy masseuse asks him to strip to his boxers and lie down. She starts to massage the young man's chest – then looks down and notices his bulge. She says, "Ah, you want wank?"

"Yes please," he says.

"OK, you stay here" she says and then leaves the room.

The student thinks, "This is what gap year holidays are all about – getting tugged off by a fit Thai bird!"

Two minutes pass and he begins to get anxious about where she's got to. Another minute later the masseuse sticks her head round the door. She says, "You finish yet?"

A British couple are on holiday in Jerusalem when the man's ever-nagging wife suddenly drops dead. The undertaker says to him, "It'll cost £10,000 to have the body flown back to Britain, or we can bury her here in The Holy Land for £250."

The man says, "I'd like the body flown home."

The undertaker says, "Why spend all that money when we can offer a special burial here for a fraction of the price?"

The man says, "A bloke died here many years ago. This is where he was buried. Three days later, he rose from the dead. I'm not taking any chances."

A duck walks into a bar and asks: "Got any Bread?"
Barman: "No."
Duck: "Got any bread?"
Barman: "No."
Duck: "Got any bread?"
Barman: "No, we have no bread."
Duck: "Got any bread?"
Barman: "No, I just said. We haven't got any bread!"
Duck: "Got any bread?"
Barman: "Are you, deaf? We haven't got any fucking bread. Ask me again and I'll nail your fucking beak to the bar!"
Duck: "Got any nails?"
Barman: "No."
Duck: "Got any bread?

Viagra is now available in powder form to put in your tea. It won't enhance your sexual performance, but it does stop your biscuits going soft.

I was just reading through that book *50 Things To Do Before You Die*, and I was really surprised that none of them was "Shout for help!"

A three-year-old was examining his testicles while taking a bath.

"Mom," he asked, "Are these my brains?"

Mother replied: "Not yet."

How many emo kids does it take to change a lightbulb?

None, they'd rather sit in the dark and cry about how everyone hates them.

George W. Bush is rehearsing a speech for the Olympics. He begins with,

"Ooo! Ooo! Ooo! Ooo! Ooo!" His assistant says, "Sir, those are the Olympic rings. Your speech starts underneath."

A little girl turns to her mum and says, "Mummy, Billy next door has a willy just like a peanut." Her mum says, "Do you mean it's really tiny?" The little girl says, "No, I mean it's really salty."

Tiger Woods drives his new Merc into an Irish petrol station. An attendant says hello but, being a bit dim, doesn't recognise him. As Woods gets out of the car, two tees fall out of his pocket. The attendant says, "What are those?" Woods says, "Tees. They're for resting my balls on when I drive." The attendant says, "Jesus, those fellas at Mercedes think of everything."

What do you say to a girl with no arms or legs?

"Nice tits."

A little girl turns to her mum:

"Mummy, Billy next door has a willy just like a peanut."

"Do you mean it's really tiny?" her mum asks.

"No," the little girl says "I mean it's really salty."

What does an Essex girl say after having sex?
"What team do you guys play for?"

A Polish immigrant in Britain decides to go for an eye test.

After working his way down to the bottom line on the chart – CZWIXNOSTACZ – the optician says: "Well, can you read that?"

"Read it?" replies the Pole. "I went to school with his brother."

A sad-looking bloke walks into a pub and sits at the bar, glumly sipping whisky. The barman asks him what's the matter.

"My life is awful," the man says. "Every night, I play Trivial Pursuit with my wife, and every night she beats me."

"Well, why don't you just stop playing Trivial Pursuit?" the barman asks.

"I love the game," the man says. "I'm a genius. I never lose."

The barman's confused. "I thought you just said your wife beats you."

"Well," the man says, "she's a bad loser."

A bloke queues in Tesco when he notices that the rather fit blonde behind him has just raised her hand and smiled hello to him. She looks familiar but he can't quite place where he knows her from.

So he says, "Sorry do you know me?"

She replies, "I may be mistaken, but I think you might be the father of one of my children."

His mind shoots back to the one and only time he's been unfaithful to his wife. "Christ!" he says "Don't tell me you're that stripper from my stag night? The one I shagged on the snooker table in front of my mates, whilst the other stripper whipped me and stuck a cucumber up my ass?"

"No," she replies, "I'm your son's English teacher."

A man suggests to his missus, "Darling, shall we try swapping positions tonight?"

"Great idea," she replies. "You stand by the ironing board while I sit on the sofa and fart."

A man walks into a bar and orders a triple scotch. As the barman pours it, he remarks, "That's quite a heavy drink. What's the problem?"

After quickly downing it, the man replies, "I found my wife in bed with my best friend."

'Wow," says the barman, giving him a refill on the house. "What did you do about it?"

"I walked over to my wife, looked her in the eye, told her to pack her stuff and get the hell out."

"That makes sense," nods the barman. "And what about your best friend?"

"I looked him right in the eye and yelled, "Bad dog.""

I asked my wife what she wanted for her birthday and she replied: "Something to run around in." So I brought her a tracksuit.

What's the difference between a Ritz biscuit and a lesbian? One's a snack cracker, the other's a crack snacker.

Teacher notices little Billy is not paying attention during maths class. Trying to catch him out she shouts out to him, "Billy, what's 9 and 15 and 37?"

Quick as a flash Billy shouts back, "Sky One, Discovery and BBC News 24, Miss"

A doctor sits one of his female patients down and with a stern look on his face says, "I'm sorry to say the tests you had don't look good. It seems that you're suffering from both cancer and Alzheimer's disease."

To which the lady replies, "Well, at least I don't have cancer!"

INTERNATIONAL

"The most famous football player in the world, Michael Beckham."

Commentator on US TV channel ABC

"Not really a loss not having the Swiss on your side in a war, is it? See the little knives they carry? 'Woah, back off, he's got some tweezers…'"

Ricky Gervais

"This is the first time in my lifetime that Irish people are able to go: 'What? You're going to England? It's full of terrorists. Come to Ireland. We've no terrorists at all. They're all playwrights now.'"

Dara Ó Briain

"North Korea and Japan have never got on. I don't think they ever will. You know what the problem is? Neither side can say sorry."

Jimmy Carr

"Unlike Englishmen, I don't need to drink alcohol before I can dance. It's natural to me, it's what I do. I'm the best dancer and the best dresser at Man United"

Cristiano Ronaldo makes himself ever more lovable

"Americans are building a new tower on the site of the World Trade Centre and looking at ways of making it terrorist-proof. They should just build a giant mosque. They wouldn't fly into that. Or, even better, a runway."

Frankie Boyle

"Italians. Slanty little eyes. Oh no, that's italics."

Milton Jones

"My top tip for World Cup commentary? Don't start speaking until at least five seconds after a national anthem. It might not be finished."

ITV's Clive Tydlesley. His other tip? "Don't mention the war"

"It is cool. It means people think about me. Now I have the recognition I deserve."

Hakan Yakin's chuffed to be named "most arrogant player"
in the Swiss league

"In my country you must be at least 18-year-old for watch scenes containing uncaged women and for view explicit sexytime you must be at least three"

Borat on film ratings in Kazakhstan

"They say travel broadens the mind, except with Americans, where it tends to widen the arse."

Jimmy Carr

"I struggle to understand English women because they talk too fast, so I just give them my number and then they go away."

Senegalese striker Henri Camara

"There are two taps over here, one for hot and one for cold. At home we have one tap for both. Also, I don't know why you have carpet in the bathroom."

Polish import Grzegorz Rasiak on his troubles settling in Southampton

"I still don't get cricket. It's difficult to understand a game that lasts five days and has a tea-time."

Thierry Henry explains the limits to his Englishness

I think Iran and Iraq simply had a war as their names are so similar they kept getting each other's post.

Paul Merton, Have I Got News For You

"Irish people love Muslims. They have taken a lot of heat off us. Before, we were The Terrorists but now, we're The Riverdance People."

Andrew Maxwell

What do you say to a German with a good-looking woman on his arm?

Nice tattoo.

LAUGHTER LINES

"In this country we spend as much on food in one week as a family in the Third World does in a year. I just can't help but think we're being overcharged for our groceries."

Jimmy Carr

"God created the Universe and man on day one. And then, on the second day, he created light. So he did all that in the dark – how cool is that?"

Ricky Gervais

"All those who believe in psychokinesis, raise my hand."

Steven Wright

"There's a condition called Pogonophobia, which is the irrational fear of beards. But is it for people who are scared of people with beards, or are they scared that a big beard is going to creep into their house with a giant magnifying glass, set fire to itself and burn all your receipts for the financial year?"

Bill Bailey

"I've got a friend who used to self-harm because he was bullied. I used to think 'whose side are you on?'"

Jimmy Carr

"TV weather bugs me, like when they put cloud and lightning on the board. I know what clouds look like! Just tell me – I'll understand!"

Billy Connolly

"Two cannibals eating a clown. One says to the other, 'Does this taste funny to you?'"

Tommy Cooper

"I don't do enough for charity. I do it a bit, but you can always do more. But I look at it like this – it's a pain, isn't it?"

Ricky Gervais

"Those people who get implants, it's so depressing. The root of that is they want more attention, but they always go for the most obvious place. If you really want more attention, why not get implants in your eyes, and then move your eyes down to where your nipples used to be, put your breasts upon your head. Everybody will pay attention."

Dylan Moran

"Cutting carrots with the Grim Reaper? That's just dicing with death."

Tim Vine

"I'm useless with technology. I bought a waterbed once, but I left my electric blanket on. I woke up poached."

Jasper Carrot

"I live quite near a special school. There's a sign on the road outside that says 'SLOW CHILDREN'. I thought, 'That can't be good for their self-esteem'. But then again, none of them can read."

Jimmy Carr

"Have you ever wondered why, when you're sick, there's always diced carrots in it? I've never eaten diced carrots in my life. I've come to the conclusion that it's not drink that makes you sick – it's diced bloody carrots."

Billy Connolly

"Genius is 10% inspiration and 90% respiration. You'd be surprised how many geniuses forget to breathe."

Stephen Colbert

"I always keep a lighter in my pocket. I don't smoke, I just like certain slow songs."

Jimmy Carr

"What's the odd one out – 15, 20, 25, 27, 30, 35 or 40? You don't need to be Carol Vorderman to say the obvious answer is 27, but you'd be wrong – it's actually 30. All the others come with fried rice."

Tam Cowan

"I said to the taxi driver, 'King Arthur's Close.' He said, 'Don't worry, we'll lose him at the next set of lights.'"

Tommy Cooper

"I come from a very traditional family. When I was seven, my Uncle Terry hanged himself on Christmas Eve. My family didn't take his body down until the sixth of January."

Nick Doody

"What they don't tell you about taking acid is that it's dull. But all these TV reviewers use it as a metaphor for shows that are wacky. 'It's like *Terry And June* on acid.' Can you imagine that? It'll be Terry staring at the floral pattern on a plate for four days."

Bill Bailey

"I like magic mushrooms but I hate mushrooms. Why can't God make magic peas instead?"

Steve Hughes

"A woman with a clipboard came up to me in the street and asked if I could spare a few minutes for cancer research. I said, 'Fine, but we won't get much done.'"

Jimmy Carr

"In ice skating, why's it called a camel spin? I've never seen a camel go round and round on one leg on ice."

Alan Davies

"Cannabis was going to be decriminalised but then it was declassified so it's now roughly the same as a strong onion."

Bill Bailey

"Let's hear it for my wife's Aunt Rosie, who was 80 yesterday. I only realised she was that old when I told a knock-knock joke and she refused to answer until I'd shown three different types of ID. Last week, she said: 'The best present I could ask for is to be surrounded by my pals.' So we took her to the cemetery."

Tam Cowan

"I saw a naked man running down the street with a woman on his back. I asked, 'Where you going?' He said, 'Fancy dress party.' 'What as?' 'A tortoise.' 'Who's that?' 'It's Michelle.'"

Peter Kay

"Parents say stupid things, don't they? 'Can I go out on my bike?' 'What? Bike? I'll give you bike!' 'But I've already got a bike...'"

Billy Connolly

"There's so many cookery shows on telly that you can't get away from them. I got a thing to apply for my new TV license in the post, and I thought fuck it, I'll just buy a cookbook."

Jack Dee

"The airlines are saying no more hair gels, shampoos, make-up or hair spray allowed in carry-on bags. Who's attacking us? Drag queens?"

Jay Leno

"Police arrested two kids yesterday. One was drinking battery acid, the other was eating fireworks. They charged one and let the other one off."

Tommy Cooper

"Know who I blame for the rise of drugs in schools? The supply teachers."

Jimmy Carr

"A policeman pulled me over and said, 'Would you please blow into this bag, sir?' I said, 'What for, Officer?' He says, 'My chips are too hot.'"

Tommy Cooper

"I went to a restaurant yesterday, and ordered my meal in French. Surprised everyone – it was a Chinese restaurant."

Tommy Cooper

"Friend of mine, Irish chap, opened a fish and chip shop. Customer walked in and asked for fish and chips twice. Fella said, 'I heard you the first time.'"

Ronnie Corbett

"I bought my son an asylum seeker doll for Christmas. It's fucking brilliant, it hangs off the back of his train set as it goes round the track."

Roy 'Chubby' Brown

"I was a pathetic drunk. I'd get so drunk that when the cops pulled me over I'd start dancing to their lights, thinking I'd made it to another club."

Bill Hicks

"This waiter brought me my lobster last night. I said, 'Just a minute, it's only got one claw.' He said, 'It's been in a fight.' I said, 'Well, bring me the winner.'"

Tommy Cooper

"Wearing a Nazi costume wasn't he cleverest thing Prince Harry's ever done. Putting himself forward as a member of the Master Race with ginger hair and only one O-level."

Graham Norton

"I'll always remember the first girl I held. You never forget your first hostage."

Jimmy Carr

"Andy Murray has agreed a £1million sponsorship with Highland Spring. But he's not the first tennis legends to sign deals with mineral water companies. I'm talking, of course, about Fred Perrier and Evian Lendl. And what about the Spanish woman giving birth to twins at age 67? Apparently she's ruled out breastfeeding. She's scared they'll get germs off the floor."

Tam Cowan

[To bloke in the audience] "Do you believe in God, sir? No?
I don't blame you, you've been dealt a very poor hand."

Harry Hill

"I phoned a takeaway last week and asked, 'Do you deliver?'
They said, 'No, we do chicken, beef and fish.'"

Peter Kay

"I bumped into a friend coming out of the doctor. 'You look
sad,' I said. He said, 'I've been diagnosed as a kleptomaniac.'
'So what did the doctor say?' 'He's given me some tablets. If
they don't work, can I get him a CD player.'"

Ronnie Corbett

**"All women have a skeleton in
the closet. All women. Even the
shy, quiet ones. Some of them got
cemeteries. You open the door and
ravens and shit fly out."**

Eddie Murphy

"My father died while fucking. He came and went at the
same time."

Richard Pryor

"We got so much food in America, we're even allergic to
it. How could someone be allergic to food? Do you think
anybody in Rwanda's lactose intolerant?"

Chris Rock

"I was on the cover of the *Big Issue* so I had to buy it. The guy said, 'I love you in *Phoenix Nights*.' I said, 'How've you seen it? I'll have my pound back, you devious bastard.'"

Peter Kay

"My feet are killing me. Every night, I wake up and they've got me round the throat."

Tommy Cooper

"I'm not going into a whole thing about how I hate garages. I think a lot of things they do are wonderful. I think it's great the way they provide black buckets for your dead flowers."

Jack Dee

"I sent my daughter to a private school. That's 73 grand's worth of education. And now she wants to be an actor? I've asked her to do porn and give me the money back."

Janey Godley

"Why did the Scots invent steam trains? So they could leave. They invented TV so they could look at other places."

Al Murray

"I'm on a whisky diet. Last week I lost three days."

Tommy Cooper

"I like to melt together four Chunky Kit-Kats so when you eat them you can pretend you're a tiny pixie."

Bill Bailey

"Dom Joly was at school with Bin Laden and still remembers those happy playground games like Tag, Stuck In The Mud and Die Infidel Die."

Angus Deayton, Would I Lie To You?

"I've had a difficult couple of weeks. I grew a beard. It turned out to be ginger. Bit disappointing. Only acceptable form of racism on the planet and I grew it on my face."

Alistair Barrie, stand-up

"I feel sorry for whales – they live in the sea and breathe air. That's like us walking with a big tank of water on your head. And they keep trying to get ashore, but we keep pushing them back."

Lee Evans

"Michael Jackson's claiming racism. Honey, you got to pick a race first."

Robin Williams

"We don't need gun control, we need bullet control. If every bullet cost $5,000, people would think before they shot someone. 'Man, if I could afford to, I would blow your fucking head off. I'm a get me another job, I'm gonna work overtime and then you're a dead man. You better hope I can't get no bullets on credit.'"

Chris Rock

"I woke up in the ambulance and there was nothing but white people staring at me. I was like, 'Ain't this a bitch, I died and ended up in the wrong heaven.'"

Richard Pryor

"I'm not homophobic. I'm not afraid of my house."

Peter Kay

"Women have this weird myth that you can tell the way a guy is in bed by how he is on a dance-floor. That's ludicrous. If a guy's on a dance-floor getting into it and enjoying himself and expressing himself, what does it matter how he is in bed? He's gay."

Bill Hicks

"Men can't say to a woman, 'You aren't fat.' You try, but it never comes out like that. It comes out like: 'You remind me distinctly of a hippo.' Or: 'There is something of the airship about you.' Or: 'I shall call you Rotunda.'"

Alan Davies

"An Iraqi judge officially dropped all remaining charges against Saddam. That's nice. You don't want to leave a guy hanging."

Jay Leno

"Vodafone say they're the word's largest mobile community. Now, correct me if I'm wrong, but that's the gypsies."

Jimmy Carr

"Nobody ever dares make Cup-a-soup in a bowl."

Peter Kay

"Hairdryers are already blowing and yet people wave them like that. What's that for? To get more wind?"

Lee Evans

"President Bush wants to set up a national database of convicted sex offenders on the internet. Don't we have this already? It's called MySpace."

Jay Leno

"I get broody, like everybody else, but when I do, I set my alarm clock to go off every hour throughout the night, cover all my favourite stuff in snot and jam, and set fire to £500. Then the feeling goes."

Jeff Green

"If your surname's 'Dumpty', don't call your first-born 'Humpty'. He probably jumped off that wall."

Ricky Gervais

"If you drop a Bible on a field mouse, it'll kill it. So maybe the Bible's not all good after all."

Harry Hill

"So I was shopping at Ikea and decided to grab a ham sandwich from the kiosk. They gave me two slices of bread, a chunk of ham, an Allen key and told me to construct it myself. It was nice. The key was gritty but went down OK."

Darren Casey

"People think I'm on drugs but I'm not. When I *am* on drugs, I'm like, 'Have you ever thought about insurance? Or a nice sensible pension plan…' But thimbles are what I really wanted to talk about. They don't get enough press these days. You rarely see a headline like: '"THIMBLES? WHOA!" SAYS MAN'. My gran said, 'Put a thimble on your finger and it helps in case you slip with your needle and it goes up, into brain, death.' Because before thimbles were invented, it was always NEEDLE DEATH TRAGIC WHOLE FAMILY! 'IF ONLY THIMBLES WERE INVENTED,' SAYS PSYCHIC MAN WITH BIG HAT. AND BEARD TO MATCH."

Eddie Izard

"I had a mate whose dream was to be run over by a steam train. It happened last week. Chuffed to bits, he was."

Tim Vine

"You girls would never help us boys out. You'd never undo the top button of your jeans. It was like trying to stroke a dog through a letterbox."

Jeff Green

"You know when people say they've been abducted by aliens, they always describe them, and it's always the same. A big head and big black eyes. I wonder if, rather than being abducted by aliens, they've actually been abducted by pandas. You've been abducted by pandas… you lie and say aliens! But at night, when darkness falls, the nightmares return… 'No, Chi Chi, nooo! No more bamboo!'"

Harry Hill

"Fat people say, 'It's glandular.' It's not glandular, is it? It's greed… And how come fat people get the same baggage allowance on flights as everyone else? 'Sorry, no bags. You spent your 50kg on your tits.'"

Ricky Gervais

"I saw an 'L' key get stuck on a typewriter, started churning out Welsh: or as I prefer to call it, 'code'."

Al Murray

"I got talking to a cab driver the other day. He told me 'I love this job, I'm on my own boss, nobody tells me what to do.' I said, 'Left here.'"

Jimmy Carr

"I finally saw *The 40 Year Old Virgin*. It was a line of guys waiting for the Playstation 3."

Jay Leno

"They can be vicious, voles. They look nice, they look like they could be one of the supporting cast in *The Wind In The Willows*. They were right to the last recall – there was Mole, Badger and Toad of course, and Vole, he'd done a little bit of fringe theatre work. He thought he'd got it, then they wrote him out of the script at the last minute. There was meant to be some sexual tension between him and the badger. The crusty old badger going, "Toad, who's that young fellow you've brought along? He's nice…" Toad: "That's my friend the vole!" Badger: "Ooh, come over here and let me have a look you… Arrrgh! God, he's a vicious bastard, isn't he? He went for my little badger arms." Perhaps he'd tried to touch his vole arse. Do they have arses? Of course they do. Not a pronounced arse. But all creatures have arses. Well, jellyfish probably don't, but little animals that you find in the woodlands have a little area just above the legs and before the back which can be touched up by an amorous badger."

Ross Noble

"A woman came from the parish council and asked me if I wanted to run a half marathon. And I said, 'Oh no, I couldn't do a half marathon.' And she said, 'You really should think about it. It's for partially sighted and blind children.' So I thought, 'Well, fuck it, I could win that.'"

Dave Spikey

"I think drowning would be a horrible way to die, but maybe a little less horrible if you're really thirsty. That's why when I'm on a boat, I bring a life jacket but also a bag of crisps. If we're going down, I say 'Give me those crisps, I'm going down parched.'"

Demetri Martin

"What's red and sits in the corner? A naughty bus."

David Mitchell, That Mitchell And Webb Look

"I used to think the brain was the greatest organ in the human body. Then I thought, 'Hey! Look what's telling me that!'"

Emo Philips,

193

"There's a lot of controversy over gay people adopting. I would have loved to have a gay dad. Remember all that stuff at school? 'My dad'll batter your dad' 'No, my dad'll batter your dad.' 'Listen, my dad'll *shag* your dad.'"

Frankie Boyle

"Employee of the month is a good example of how somebody can be both a winner and a loser at the same time."

Demetri Martin

"So I said to my personal trainer 'Can you teach me to do the splits?'
   He said 'How flexible are you?'
   I said 'I can't make Tuesdays.'"

Peter Kay

"An air steward at Glasgow Airport set off a security alert after overhearing a man say he was a Basque terrorist. Turns out it was Adam Clayton from U2. He said he was a bass guitarist."

Tam Cowan

"I went out the other day, and bought some blond hair and a pair of blue eyes. I'm saving them for the right Caucasian."

Tim Vine

"When the kids in the playground discovered I had a possibly fatal allergy to peanuts, they'd to push me up against the wall and make me play Russian roulette with a packet of Revels."

Milton Jones

"I got an odd-job man in. He was useless. Gave him a list of eight things to do and he only did numbers one, three, five and seven. Had to get an even-man in to finish it off."

Stephen Grant

"I used to go to the playground and watch all the children run and scream… They didn't know I was using blanks."

Emo Phillips

"Christmases were terrible as a poor kid. My sister got a miniature set of perfumes called Ample. Even I could see where my dad had scraped off the S."

Stephen K. Amos

"I'd rather see a pregnant girl standing up on a bus, than a fat girl sitting down, crying."

Jimmy Carr

"The worst time to have a heart attack is during a game of charades. Especially if the other players are bad guessers. 'Fat Guy On The Floor? I've never seen THAT movie.'"

Demetri Martin

"Jesus was a carpenter. A tradesman. You can tell he was a tradesman because he disappeared off the face of the earth for three days with no rational explanation."

Al Murray

"So I rang up a local building firm and said, 'I want a skip outside my house.' He said, 'I'm not stopping you.'"

Tim Vine

"Steven Hawking's not a genius. He's pretentious. Born in Kent and talks with an American accent."

Ricky Gervais

"I used to go jogging. I went four miles a day. I did it for two weeks. I got so fucking far away from my house I couldn't get back."

Lee Evans

"Health experts reckon laughing for 15 minutes a day could win the war against obesity. So now you know why Dawn French (aka Mrs Lenny Henry) is the size of a Number 67 bus."

Tam Cowan

"When I was a kid, I asked my mother: 'Mum, what's a transvestite?'
    She said, 'That's your father, I'm over here.'"

Adrian Poynton

"The average American car weighs 500lbs more than it did ten years ago. Of course, that's only true if the average American is sitting in it."

Conan O'Brien, US chat show host

"My pyjamas have pockets. They're really useful, because now I don't have to carry stuff while I sleep."

Demetri Martin

"If we didn't have rules, where would we be? France."

Al Murray

"If guys could blow themselves, then ladies, you'd be alone in this room right now. Watching an empty stage."

Bill Hicks

"I was sad when they got Saddam. That's kinda like the coyote catching the Roadrunner. I guess Acme finally made some shit that worked. I didn't even know we were after Hussein. I thought we were after Bin Laden. When I heard we were after Hussein, I was like 'Really? That's so '80s.' The whole war seemed like a bad VH1 special. Hussein is back. Bush is back. Cheney is back. Paula Abdul is back. Before you know it, it'll be Hammer Time again."

Chris Rock

"Why do builders have see-through lunchboxes? So they can tell if they're going home or coming to work."

Jack Dee

"Britain didn't enter the Vietnam war because we like our war films to have happy endings."

Al Murray

"A young man having sex with an old woman is advised to treat the experience like rock climbing: stare at the craggy face and try not to glance at the horrors, beneath."

Garry Bushell

"Fat people make excuses. They say, 'I eat the occasional sweet.' Yeah, three-piece suite.'"

Ricky Gervais

"Have you noticed the way that burns victims stick together?"

Carey Marx

"You know the world is going crazy when the best rapper is white, the best golfer is black, the tallest guy in the NBA is Chinese, the Swiss hold the America's Cup, France is accusing the US of arrogance, Germany doesn't want to go to war and the three most powerful men in America are named Bush, Dick, and Colon."

Chris Rock

"I went to Wales. No bugger talks to you. I know how Kevin Costner felt in *Dances With Wolves*. Six weeks on a beach, on my own, sitting there, being feared by the locals. Until eventually they brought me a bit of bread. And I befriended them and I started to live as one of them and for the first time in my life I was happy. And I thought, 'Why bother doing this stand-up shit when I can be here and be loved for who I am.' And I'd have stayed there. But I made the fatal mistake of buying some Coco Pops. Which, I don't know if you know, turn the milk brown. I was nearly burnt as a fucking witch. I'm sitting there eating me breakfast and they're building a wicker man in the back garden. I had to flee for me life dressed a sheep. Do you know how hard it is making a credible sheep noise while some fucker's taking you roughly from behind? 'BAAAAAA!' I broke down, I couldn't help it. 'Could you be more gentle!' Farmer shat himself. I was dragged back to the village as a local oddity. Everyone's going, 'I don't see what's so special about him.' Farmer's going, 'Wait till you fuck him – he talks!' I spent six weeks tied up in the village square, with every dozy bastard having a go at me... [Makes pelvis-thrusting motions] 'Come on, tell me fortune.' 'You'll never marry...'"

Johnny Vegas

TV SHOWS

"America's favourite pastime starts again. It's that season again when big sweaty guys start grabbing their crotches, yelling and swinging baseball bats – yes, *The Sopranos* is back."

Craig Ferguson, US talkshow host

"If your parents are getting divorced, it can be a very traumatic time. Don't worry – it's not your fault. Your mum's a slag."

Jimmy Carr, 8 Out Of 10 Cats

"Did you know that 60 per cent of all cosmetic surgery patients are disappointed with the results? Though they look pleasantly surprised."

Jimmy Carr, 8 Out of 10 Cats

"40,000 Americans are injured in the toilet every year, mostly accidents from slipping on a wet floor. It just goes to show: you've got to look out for number 1."

Jimmy Carr, 8 Out of 10 Cats

"A new study shows that eating salmon is not only good for you, but makes you happier. However, some experts disagree: grizzly bears."

Saturday Night Live

"George Bush is now also worried about global warming, but he has a plan. He's going to invade the sun."

David Letterman, The Late Show

"The government is worried about the growing number of people subscribing to suicide websites. Subscribing? Surely it's cheaper to pay as you go?"

Alan Carr, The Friday Night Project

"Muse's equipment was destroyed by high winds at the aptly-named Hurricane Festival in Germany recently. I can only wish them the best of luck when they play at this year's World AIDS Day"

Simon Amstell, Never Mind The Buzzcocks

"A guy walks into a dentist's office and says, 'I think I'm a moth.' The dentist says, 'Well, if you think you're a moth, why did you come to the dentist's office?' The guy says, 'Well, the light was on.'"

JD, Scrubs

"I put my air conditioner in backwards. It got cold outside. The weatherman on TV was confused. It was supposed to be hot today."

Steven Wright

South Park

Cartman (after a goat is sent to him): It's an Afghanistan goat, so it can't stay here, or else it'll choke on the sweet air of freedom.

Kyle: Wow, that's a lot of semen Cartman.
    Cartman: Yeah. I got it from this guy Ralph in an alley. And the sweet thing is, the stupid asshole didn't even charge me money for it. He just made me close my eyes and suck it out of a hose.

Wendy: Dude, dolphins are intelligent and friendly!"
    Cartman: If they're so smart, how come they live in igloos? Intelligent and friendly on rye bread with mayo please.

Cartman: Independent films are those black and white hippy movies. They're always about gay cowboys eating pudding.

Kyle: I hate being small and Jewish. I feel like a tall black man.
    Plastic surgeon: You need a negroplasty. It's a fairly common procedure. Just the reverse of a caucasioplasty like Michael Jackson had.

Paris Hilton: I'm pleased to be here in Douth Dark to open my brand new store. A store where girls can buy everything they need to be just like me: Stupid Spoiled Whore.

Mr Garrison: Now does anyone know what sexual harassment means? Yes, Eric?

Cartman: When you're trying to have intercourse with a lady friend and some other guy comes up and tickles your balls from behind.

Mr Garrison: Genetic engineering is a way to fix God's horrible mistakes, like German people.

Seinfeld

Jerry: Looking at cleavage is like looking at the sun. You don't stare at it. It's too risky. You get a sense of it and then you look away.

George [on dating a woman in jail]: Jerry, I like being with her. Plus, I know where she is all the time. I have relatively no competition. And you know how you live in fear of the pop-in? No "in the neighbourhood," no "I saw your light was on."

George: She calls me up at my office, she says, "We have to talk."

Jerry: Ugh, the four worst words in the English language.

George: That, or "Whose bra is this?"

George: When do you start to worry about ear hair?

Jerry: When you hear, like, a soft rustling.

George: Who buys an umbrella anyway? You can get them for free at the coffee shop, by the door in those metal cans.

Jerry: Those belong to people.

Jerry: Breaking up is like knocking over a Coke machine. You can't do it in one push, you got to rock it back and forth a few times, and then it goes over.

George: Why go to funerals? You think dead people care who's at the funeral? They don't even know they're having a funeral. It's not like she's hanging out in the back going, "I can't believe Jerry didn't show up".

Elaine: Maybe she's there in spirit.

George: If you're a spirit, and you can travel to other dimensions and galaxies, and find out the mysteries of the universe, you think you'll want to hang around Drexler's funeral home on Ocean Parkway?

Family Guy

Chris: Dad, what's the whale's blowhole for?

Peter: I'll tell you what it's not for, son. And when I do, you'll understand why I can never go back to Sea World.

Lois: I care about the size of your penis as much as you care about the size of my breasts.

Peter: Oh my God! (runs off crying).

Peter: OK, here's another riddle. A woman has two children.

A psycho killer tells her she can only keep one. Which one does she let him kill?

    Brian: That's not a riddle. That's just terrible.

    Peter: Wrong, the ugly one!

Brian: Who the hell buys a novelty fire extinguisher?

    Peter: I'll tell you who. Someone who cares enough about physical comedy to put his whole family at risk.

Lois, watching a sexy beer ad: I guarantee you a man made that commercial.

    Peter: Of course a man made it. It's a commercial, Lois, not a delicious thanksgiving dinner.

Stewie (to a prostitute): So, is there any tread left on the tyres? Or would it be like throwing a hotdog down a hallway?

Lois: Honey, what do you say we uh…christen these new sheets, huh?

    Peter: Why Lois Griffin, you naughty girl.

    Lois: Hehehe…that's me.

    Peter: You dirty hustler.

    Lois: Hehehehe…

    Peter: You filthy, stinky prostitute.

    Lois: Aha, ok I get it…

    Peter: You foul, venereal disease carrying, street walking whore.

    Lois: Alright, that's enough!

Futurama

Amy Wong: You just have to give guys a chance. Sometimes you meet a guy and think he's a pig, but then later on you realize he actually has a really good body.

Fry: Ooh. "Big Pink." It's the only gum with the breath-freshening power of ham.

Soldier: This is the worst part. The calm before the battle.
   Fry: And then the battle is not so bad?
   Soldier: Oh, right. I forgot about the battle.

Bender: Hey, what kind of party is this? There's no booze and only one hooker.

Fry: Man, I thought Ultimate Robot Fighting was real, like pro wrestling, but it turns out it's fixed, like boxing.

Oscar Presenter: And the nominees for Best Soft Drink Product Placement are… Star Trek: The Pepsi Generation, They Call Me Mr. Pibb, and Snow White and the Seven-ups.

Nibblonian: You are the last hope of the universe.
Fry: So I really am important? How I feel when I'm drunk is correct?
   Nibblonian: Yes – except the Dave Matthews Band doesn't rock.

Bender: You're watching *Futurama*, the show that doesn't condone the cool crime of robbery.

Captain Zapp Brannigan: If we hit that bullseye, the rest of the dominoes should fall like a house of cards. Checkmate.

The Simpsons

Chief Wiggum: "No, you have the wrong number. This is 91… 2."

Homer to Bart: These three little sentences will get you through life. "Oh good idea boss!" "Cover for me". "It was like that when I got here"

Scully from the *X-Files*: This is a simple lie detector test. I'll ask you a few yes-or-no questions and you just answer truthfully. Do you understand?
   Homer: Yes. [Lie detector explodes]

Homer: I saw this movie about a bus that had to speed around the city, keeping its *speed* over fifty. And if its speed dropped, the bus would explode. I think it was called, *The Bus That Couldn't Slow Down*.

Mr Burns: Oh, so Mother Nature needs a favour? Well, maybe she should have thought of that when she was besetting us with droughts and floods and poison monkeys.

Homer: Every time I learn something new it pushes some old stuff outta my brain. Remember when I took that wine tasting lesson and I forgot how to drive?

Marge (on radio): Husband on murderous rampage. Send help. Over.

Chief Wiggum: Phew, thank God it's over. I was worried for a little bit.

Homer: Maybe, just once, someone will call me "sir" without adding, "you're making a scene."

Homer (pointing at Uruguay on a globe): "Look at this country: U R Gay."

Mr Burns: "You'd kneel before me, wouldn't you Smithers?"
Smithers: "Boy, would I."

Ralph Wiggum: "Me fail English? That's unpossible!"

Lionel Hutz (talking about the judge): Well, he's kind of had it in for me ever since I accidentally ran over his dog. Actually, replace "accidentally" with "repeatedly," and replace "dog" with "son.

TOP TENS

Top Ten Hybrid Animals

1 TIGON/LIGER

A male tiger/female lion (tigon) and vice versa for a liger. Liger's are the world's largest cats, with some standing 12ft tall on their hind legs and weigh around half a ton.

2 WOLF DOG

Dogs and wolves crossbreed freely, and this is the result. The jaws are stronger than a dog, but they can still be domesticated and obedience trained.

3 IRON AGE PIG

Domestic Tamworth pigs crossed with wild boars. Tamer than boars, but still bred only for specialist pork sausages.

4 ZEBROID

The general term for zebra crosses. Specifically, a zorse is zebra/horse, a zonkey is zebra/donkey and a zony crosses zebra with pony.

5 CAMA

Camel and a llama. Born via artificial insemination due to the size difference. Sadly, the hump gets lost on the process.

6 GROLAR/PIZZLY

When polar bears and grizzlies meet and do sex. The bears are genetically similar, but tend to avoid each other in the wild. In April 2006 a hunter managed to shoot one in Canada. So while we know they exist, we blew away the only one that came close.

7 LEOPON

The bastard child of a male leopard and female lion. They like to "climb and enjoy water". A successful breeding program exists in Japan.

8 HYBRID PHEASANT

The colourful result of a golden pheasant crossed with a lady Amherst's pheasant

9 WOLPHIN

Take a bottlenose dolphin and a killer whale and let them at it. This is the result. Currently there are just two in captivity, in Hawaii's Sea Life Park.

10 TI-LIGER, TI-TIGON, LI-TIGON, LI-LIGER

The ultimate! A hybrid among hybrids. Crossbreeding between male tiger and female liger/tigon or male lion with female tigon/liger. Only a few examples exist in specialist research facilities.

Top Ten Most Promiscuous Nations By The Amount Of Times People Have Sex A Year

1. Greece 138
2. Croatia 134
3. Serbia & Montenegro 128
4. Bulgaria 127
5. Czech Republic 120 = France 120
7. United Kingdom 118
8 Netherlands 115 = Poland 115
10 United States 114

(www.durex.com)

Top Ten Most Expensive Bits Of Football Memorabillia

1. The FA Challenge Cup (1896–1910)
   £478,400
2. Jules Rimet replica trophy
   £254,000
3. Alan Ball's 1966 World Cup Winner's medal 2005
   £164,800
4. Pele's shirt from the 1970 World Cup Final 2002
   £157,750
5. Part of ex-Wolves and England captain Billy Wright's medal collection 1996
   £134,550
6. Gordon Banks 1966 World Cup Winner's medal 2001
   £124,750
7. Collection of medals, caps and shirts awarded to Ray Kennedy 1993
   £101,200

8. Geoff Hurst's red shirt from the 1966 World Cup Final
   2001
   £91,750
9. Ray Wilson's 1966 World Cup Winner's medal 2002
   £80,750
10. Pele's shirt from the 1958 World Cup Final 2004
   £70,505

Top 10 UK Fetishes

1. Leather/rubber/latex/vinyl
2. Feet/hands
3. Domination/submission
4. Stomachs
5. Body piercing
6. Fingernails/lipstick
7. Braids/ponytails/pigtails
8. Water
9. Voyeurism/exhibitionism
10. Golden Showers

Top Ten Last Words

1 "I should never have switched from Scotch to Martinis."
   Humphrey Bogart (1899–1957)
2 "These curtains are killing me; one of us has got to go."
   Oscar Wilde (1854–1900)
3 *Adieu, mes amis, je vais à la gloire!* (Farewell my friends,
   I go to glory!)
   Isadora Duncan (1877–1927)

4 "Damn it… Don't you dare ask God to help me."
   Joan Crawford (1905–1977) to her maid began praying

5 "Hurry up, you Hoosier bastard; I could kill 10 men while you're fooling around!"
   Carl Panzram (1891–1930) prior to his execution

6 "Don't let it end like this. Tell them I said something."
   Pancho Villa (1878–1923)

7 "I did not know that we had ever quarreled."
   Henry David Thoreau (1817–1862) when urged to make peace with God

8 "I'm warning you boys, I'm a screamer."
   Davy Crockett (1786–1836), prior to his execution

9 "Now, now, my good man, this is no time for making enemies."
   Voltaire (1694–1778), when asked to renounce Satan

10 "Thank God. I'm tired of being the funniest person in the room."
   Del Close (1934–1999)

Source: www.askmen.com

Top Ten Most Spectacular Comebacks

1. *Escape to Victory*, Allies vs Germany 1944.
   Allies 4–0 down after 41 minutes but come back to draw 4–4.

2. Liverpool vs AC Milan, Champions League Final 2005.
   3–0 down at half-time, Reds come back to draw 3–3 and win on penalties.

3. Manchester City vs Tottenham, FA Cup 2004. City were 3–0 down but come back to win 4–3 at White Hart Lane.

4. USSR vs Yugoslavia, 1952 Olympics. The Yugoslavians leading 5–1 early in the second half. The Russians come back to draw 5–5.

5. Deportivo La Coruna vs Real Madrid, Champions League quarter-final 2004. La Coruna were 4–1 down after the first leg but take Milan apart at the Riazor 4–0 to go through.

6. Partizan Belgrade vs QPR, Uefa Cup 2nd Round, 1984. QPR tear the Yugoslavs apart at Loftus Road, winning the 1st leg 6–2. Then lose the return leg 4–0 and go out on the away goal.

7. Portugal vs North Korea, World Cup quarter-final, 1966. Eusabio's lot find themselves 3–0 down to Korea before reverting to type and winning 5–3

8. Bayern Munich vs Bayern Uerdingen, German Cup 1986. Munich are 5–1 down on aggregate with 33 minutes left but galvanize themselves somehow to come back and win 7–5.

9. West Germany vs England, World Cup quarter-final 1970. England, the World Champions are cruising and two up with 20 minutes left. Nauseatingly, the Germans fight back to win 3-2 and we've never recovered.

10. Tottenham vs Southampton, FA Cup 5th Round, 1995. Spurs are two down at half-time but hit back at the Dell with 6 2nd half goals, including a Ronny Rosenthal hat-trick.

Top Ten Oldest Scottish Distilleries

1. Glenturret 1775
2. Bowmore 1779
3. Strathisla 1786
4. Tobermory 1795
5. = Highland Park 1798
5. = Ardbeg 1798
5. = Glen Garioch 1798
8. Glenburgie 1810
9. Laphroaig 1816
10. = Lagavulin 1817
10. = Teaninich 1817

Top Ten Most Prolific Swordsmen

1. Umberto Billo (Venetian hotel porter) – 8,000
2. Charlie Sheen (actor) – 5,000
3. Gene Simmons (KISS frontman) – 4,600
4. Julio Iglesias (singer) – 3,000
   = Engelbert Humperdink (singer) – 3,000
6. Ilie Nastase – 2,500
7. Jack Nicholson (actor) – 2,000
8. Lemmy Kilmister (Motorhead frontman) – 1,200
9. Earvin 'Magic' Johnson (basketball star) – 1,000
10. Bill Wyman (ex-Rolling Stone) – 1,000

Richest Gaffers In Britain

1. Roy Keane, Sunderland £27m
2. Jose Mourniho, Chelsea £22m

3. Sir Alex Ferguson, Manchester United £20m
4. Sven Goran Eriksson (Still paid by FA) £14m
5. Harry Redknapp, Portsmouth £12m
6. Arsene Wenger, Arsenal £11m
7. Rafa Benitez, Liverpool £9
8. Martin O'Neil, Aston Villa £7m
9. Mark Hughes, Blackburn £6m
10. Steve McClaren, England £6m

Top Ten Names And Sizes Of 'Big Boob Superstars'

1. Chelsea Charms 153XXX
2. Cindy Fulsome 120QQQ
3. Plenty Uptopp 127PPP
4. Maxi Mounds 42M
5. Minka 44KK
6. Traci Topps 34JJ
7. B.B. Gunns 76HHH
8. Pandora Peaks 72HHH
9. Crystal Gunns 46GG
10. Donita Dunes 44GG

Top Ten Strongest Beers Ever brewed

1. Hair Of The Dog Dave, USA 29% ABV
2. Hakusekikan Eisbock, Japan 28%
3. Samuel Adams Utopias, USA 25%
4. Barley John's Rosie's Ale, USA 23%
5. Dogfish Head World Wide Stout, USA 22%
6. Dogfish Head 120 Minute IPA, USA 21%
7. Grand Lake Holy Grail, USA 20%

8. Samuel Adams Millennium, USA 19.5%
9. Dogfish Head "Raison d'Extra, USA 18.5%
10. Dogfish Head "Fort, USA 18%

Top 10 Best Urinals In The World (And Beyond)

1. Amundsen-Scott South Pole Station, South Pole, Antarctica
2. The Taj Mahal, Agra, Uttar Pradesh, India
3. Nature's Call by Clark Sorensen, San Francisco, USA
4. Public Rest Rooms of Rothesay, Rothesay, Isle of Bute, UK
5. Mystique Night Club – Kisses, Bangkok, Thailand
6. Women's Urinal at Dairy Queen, Port Charlotte, Florida, USA
7. Stockholm-Arlanda Airport, Stockholm, Sweden
8. International Space Station, In Space
9. John Michael Kohler Arts Center, New York, USA
10. The Felix, Hong Kong

Source: www.urinal.net

Top Ten Body Parts Injured Most Often In A Shark Attack

1. Calf/knee 34.6%
2. Arm 28.9%
3. Thigh 23.5 %
4. Foot 22.1%
5. Hand 12.8%
6. Abdomen/stomach 9.4%
7. Chest 8.7%

=8 Buttocks 7.4%

=8 Shoulder 7.4%

10. Back 6.7%

Source: International Shark Attack File, Florida Museum of Natural History

Top Ten Most League Titles In Europe

1. Glasgow Rangers 51
2. Linfield 45
3. Celtic 39
4. Olympiakos 33
5. Rapid Vienna 32
6. Benfica 31
7. CSKA Sofia 30
8. Ajax 29
9. Real Madrid 29
10. Juventus 28

Top 10 Britain's Least Rock 'n' Roll Towns

With their most musical son or daughter. As voted by rockingvicar.com

1. Milton Keynes – nobody. Fact.
2. Plymouth – ditto (but Dawn French studied there and once appeared on a Comic Relief single with Bananarama
3. Doncaster – John Parr (one-hit wonder with St Elmo's Fire)
4. Reading – Morning Runner (plus Ricky Gervais of Free Love Highway fame and a rock festival)
5. Dunstable – Faye Tozer out of Steps

6. Clacton – 80s crooning model Sade
7. Batley – Robert Palmer
8. Ipswich – Charlie out of Busted
9. Peterborough – Andy Bell out of Erasure
10. Eastbourne – Toploader

Top Ten Brands Mentioned In Songs

1. Mercedes – 100 mentions
2. Nike – 63 mentions
3. Cadillac – 62 mentions
4. Bentley – 51 mentions
5. Rolls-Royce – 46 mentions
6. Hennessy Congac – 44 mentions
7. Chevrolet – 40 mentions
8. Louis Vuitton – 35 mentions
9. Cristal champagne – 28 mentions
10. AK-47 assault rifles – 33 mentions

Source: lyrics US Top 200 singles during 2006

Top Ten British Pub Names According To CAMRA

1. The Crown, 704 pubs
   A recent number one, as more pubs called The Red Lion have closed than royalist Crowns. A popular pub name for 600 years (except for a gap during the Cromwell Commonwealth).
2. The Red Lion, 668 pubs
   When King James VI of Scotland became James I of England too in 1603, he decreed that all public buildings should display the red lion of Scotland.

3. The Royal Oak, 541 pubs
    The name comes from King Charles II's attempt to hide from the Roundheads by shinning up an oak in Shropshire, during the Civil War in 1651.

4. The Swan, 451 pubs
    Many noble families had a swan in their coat of arms, so this is often a tribute to the local landowner. In the Midlands, it often refers to Shakespeare, the "Swan of Avon".

5. The White Hart, 431 pubs
    This was 14th century king Richard II's nickname. History does not record whether he liked a pint.

6. The Railway, 420 pubs
    Most of these pubs were opened next to the new railway stations, during the Victorian growth of the steam railway.

7. The Plough, 413 pubs
    Despite pub signs often showing the constellation, this refers to agriculture. Farm hands going to The Plough after a hard day's work – that's like us going to The PC and Mobile for a pint.

8. The White Horse, 379 pubs
    Popular in Kent, because it's the county symbol; in pubs near chalk horse figures; and pubs opened in the 18th and 19th centuries, during the reign of Hanoverian monarchs (white horse crest)

9. The Bell, 378 pubs
    Usually used by pubs close to churches. Subtle hint to go and sing a hymn or two before getting ratted on a Sunday lunchtime.

10. The New Inn, 372 pubs
    Usually the second pub in a village whose population

had grown, ironically there are New Inns dating back to the 16th Century.

Top Ten Places Britons Like To Have Sex

1. Hotel room
2. Outside in the sunshine
3. Bath
4. Kitchen
5. Woods
6. Planes
7. Car
8. Weddings
9. Bed
10. The beach

Top Ten Packets Of Crisps Sold In The UK

Walkers is Britain's most popular snack brand. But which of their flavours sells best?

1. Cheese and onion crisps
2. Ready-salted crisps
3. Cheesy Quavers
4. Salt and vinegar crisps
5. Prawn cocktail crisps
6. Thai sweet chilli Sensations
7. Flamin' Hot Monster Munch
8. Pickled onion Monster Munch
9. Cheesy Wotsits
10. Roast chicken crisps

Top Ten Rejected Band Names

1. Pectoralz – Coldplay
2. Bastard – Mötorhead
3. The Rain – Oasis
4. On A Friday – Radiohead
5. Faecal Matter – Nirvana
6. Seymour – Blur
7. The Strand – The Libertines
8. The Hype – U2
9. The Lotus Eaters – Keane
10. Dead Lesbian and the Fibrillating Scissor Sisters – Scissor Sisters

Top Ten Most Expensive Cities To Live

1. Oslo, Norway
2. Tokyo, Japan
3. Reykjavik, Iceland
4. Osaka, Japan
5. Paris, France
6. Copenhagen, Denmark
7. London, England
8. Zurich, Switzerland
9. Geneva, Swtizerland
10. Helsinki, Finland

Top Ten Grossing films (Inflation Adjusted)

1. *Gone With the Wind*, $2700m
2. *Snow White and the Seven Dwarfs*, $2699m

3. *Titanic*, $2245m
4. *Star Wars Episode IV: A New Hope*, $1438m
5. *Jurassic Park*, $1236m
6. *Bambi*, $1191m
7. *The Lord of the Rings: The Return of the King*, $1187m
8. *Harry Potter and the Philosopher's Stone*, $1077m
9. *Star Wars: Episode One – The Phantom Menace*, $1054m
10. *The Lion King*, $1032m

Top Ten Pound-For-Pound Fighters In The World, According To Boxing Bible *Ring*

1. Floyd Mayweather Jnr
2. Manny Pacquiano
3. Ronaldo "Winky" Wright
4. Marco Antonio Barrera
5. Jermain Taylor
6. Bernard Hopkins
7. Oscar De La Hoya
8. Joe Calzaghe
9. Antonio Margarito
10. Ricky Hatton

Top Ten World's Most Expensive Wines... And What To Say About Them...

1. Domaine Romane Conti 1997 £775
   Rich red Burgundy: berries, soy sauce, liquorice
2. Petrus Pomerol 1998 1998 £725
   JFK's favourite wine, a Merlot

3. Chateau Le Pin Pomerol 1999 £450
   A Bordeaux with black cherry and mocha flavour
4. Chateau Latour Pauillac 1990 £380
   Given a rare perfect score by booze bible Wine Spectator
5. Chateau Valandraud Saint-Emilion 1995 £335
   Comes from a tiny French vinyard of only 35 acres
6. Chateau La Mondotte Saint-Emilion 1996 £300
   Even smaller vinyard (11 acres) producing a fruity
   number
7. Chateau Mouton Rothschild Pauillac 1986 £290
   British family vinyard, famous for labels by artists
   including Picasso and Warhol
8. Chateau Haut Brion Pessac-Lognan 1982 £265
   Chateau that produced the first ever Bordeaux wine
9. Chateau Margaux 1995 £200
   Almost black red wine from a 1,000 year-old vinyard
10. Chateau Lafite Rothschild Pauillac 1996 £150
    The favourite drink of King Louis XV of France

Top 10 Richest British Comedians

1. Tracey Ullman, £75 million
   Eighties comic has shares in *The Simpsons*, which started
   on her US show
2. Rowan Atkinson, £40 million
   No-translation-required idiot Mr Bean sells worldwide,
   plus shares in Tiger Aspect (makers of *The Vicar Of Dibley*)
3. Jasper Carrott, £35 million
   Brummie owns shares in *Who Wants To Be A Millionaire?*

4. John Cleese, £30 million
   The not-funny-since-the-therapy Python made
   made his dosh from films and his training video empire
5. = Griff Rhys-Jones, £25 million
   The ruined building-botherer made money from selling
   Talkback production company (*Partridge, Buzzcocks, Ali G*)
5. = Mel Smith, £25 million
   The big-boned balding one from *Smith & Jones* also
   made his cash flogging Talkback to Thames
7. Steve Coogan, £11 million
   Much of his cash comes from *Alan Partridge* DVDs and
   Baby Cow Productions (*Boosh, Nighty Night*)
8. Jennifer Saunders, £10 million
   From *Ab Fab* success and co-owns production company
   Mr & Mrs Monsoon with ex-*Young Ones* hubbie Ade
   Edmonson
9. Eddie Izzard, £9.5 million
   The funny tranny has stormed the USA with live tours
   and DVDs, plus roles in movies including the Ocean's
   series and Jerry Seinfeld's *Bee Movie*
10. Peter Kay, £8 million
    To the annoyance of some of his co-writers, Kay has
    raked in most of the moolah from *Phoenix Nights*, as well
    as his solo work and huge-selling memoirs

Top Ten 200mph Supercars

1. Bugatti Veyron 253mph
2. McLaren F1 240mph
3. Koenigsegg CC 8S 240mph
4. Pagani Zonda C12S 220mph
5. Ferrari Enzo 218mph
6. Jaguar XJ220 217mph
7. Bugatti EB110 209mph
8. Mercedes McLaren SLR 208mph
9. Maserati MC12 206mph
10. Porsche Carrera GT 205mph

Top Ten Average Lifetime Sexual Partners Worldwide

1. Turkey 14.5
2. Australia 13.5
3. Italy 11.8
4. Switzerland 11.1
5. USA 10.7
6. Japan 10.2
7. UK 9.8
8. Austria 9.7
9. France 8.1
10. Singapore 7.2

ONE-LINERS

"The moth. Pretty much a Seventies butterfly."

Noel Fielding

"One armed butlers, eh? They can take it – but they can't dish it out."

Tim Vine

"We've got new neighbours. He's got this German shepherd that craps on the lawn. And he's got a dog."

Jasper Carrot

"Old people. You can't beat them, can you? Pity."

Peter Kay

"Somebody complimented me on my driving today. They left a little note on the windscreen, it said, 'Parking Fine.'"

Tim Vine

"I went to a general store. They wouldn't let me buy anything specific."

Steven Wright

"Nobody thought Mel Gibson could play a Scot but look at him now: alcoholic and a racist."

Frankie Boyle

"A friend of mine died of dyslexia. He choked on his own Vimto."

Dave Spikey

"Cats have got nine lives. Which makes them ideal for experimentation."

Jimmy Carr

"I went to see a go-go dancer. But she'd gone."

Harry Hill

"What's another word for Thesaurus?"

Steven Wright

"I got thrown out of the scouts for eating a brownie."

Ross Noble

"Everyone hates you. Surely you remember that from school?"

David Baddiel's put-down to a heckler at The Comedy Store.

"Yeah I have a girlfriend. I've been going out with her for… sex."

Stewart Francis, US stand-up

"If it becomes illegal to wear the veil at work, bee-keepers will be furious."

Milton Jones

"I was reading this book called *The History of Glue*. I couldn't put it down."

Tim Vine

"Apparently you can tell a lot about people from what they're like."

Harry Hill

"I had a great business plan: I was going to build bungalows for dwarfs. There was only one tiny flaw..."

Justin Edwards

"I love to freak out shop assistants. They ask what size I need, and I say, 'Extra medium.'"

Steven Wright

"My love life is terrible. The last time I was inside a woman was when I visited the Statue of Liberty."

Woody Allen

"If you have a pear-shaped body, you shouldn't wear pear-coloured clothes. Or act juicy."

Demetri Martin

"I'll tell you what I love doing more than anything: trying to pack myself in a small suitcase. I can hardly contain myself."

Peter Kay

"As I was getting into my car, this bloke says to me 'Can you give me a lift?'
I said 'Sure, you look great, the world's your oyster, go for it.'"

Tim Vine

"The trouble with heroin is it's very moreish."

Harry Hill

"Today I met a subliminal advertising executive – but only very briefly."

Steven Wright

"My parents are from Glasgow. I was never smacked as a child. Well, maybe one or two grams to get me to sleep at night."

Susan Murray

"There'd be less litter in Britain if blind people were given pointed sticks."

Adam Bloom

"Two guys came knocking at my door once and said: 'We want to talk to you about Jesus.' I said: 'Oh, no, what's he done now?'"

Kevin McAleer

"I never sleep with fish. I'm halibut."

Tim Vine

"I don't take drugs anymore… than the average touring funk band."

Bill Hicks

"I have a really nice stepladder. Sadly, I never knew my real ladder."

Harry Hill

"Those Harry Potter films are so unrealistic. I ask you, a ginger kid with two friends."

"When my Grandad got ill, my Grandma used to rub lard into his back. He went downhill pretty fast after that."

Milton Jones

"So I met this gangster who pulls up the back of people's pants. It was Wedgie Kray."

Peter Kay

"I'm still making love at 71, which is handy for me because I live at number 63."

Bernie Clifton

"Before I got into comedy, I was a plumber for 150 years – although that's just an estimate."

Gordon Southern

"My dad used to keep Eskimos and alligators. He bred escalators. We got a lot of funny stairs."

Marek Larwood

"I was in a bookstore the other day, there was a third off all titles. I bought *The Lion, The Witch*."

Jimmy Carr

"Velcro. What a rip-off."

Tim Vine

"Disabled loos. Ironically, the only loos big enough to run around in."

Adam Bloom

"Why is it always Tudor houses we mock?"

Harry Hill

"They say being a hostage is difficult. But I could do that with my hands tied behind my back."

Phil Nichol

SEX

"I like my body and I like sex. So yeah, I'm good in bed. I used to be a dancer so I am very flexible. I'm naturally bendy. If blokes want to explore that quality, then it's up to them."

Presenter Fearne Cotton gets our minds boggling

"I fancy women big time. I check them out far more than I check out men. Maybe I'd like to sleep with a woman. But not Beyonce. I don't think she's dirty enough."

Billie Piper's probably right. But an enduring image anyhow

"British men spend on average 22 minutes on foreplay. Of course, that's spread out between all of us over the course of a year."

Jimmy Carr, 8 Out Of 10 Cats

"If a woman's performing oral sex on me, I have to admit I will have a little look down. Usually just to think, 'Ugh, how could you?'"

Frank Skinner

"My grandad died aged 93 while he was shagging my gran. I said, 'That must have been awful.'" She said, 'Not really, I were asleep.'"

Dave Spikey

"I'm not averse to being tied up in silk scarves. I like a man to take charge. There's something very sexy about being submissive."

Desperate Housewives' Eva Longoria

"My girlfriends surprised me on my 80th birthday in the grotto with 18 girls, but I don't think I had sex with all of them. Maybe 11."

Playboy tycoon Hugh Hefner

"Beware trim and tidy."
Think your missus is cheating on you? Then heed blonde sexpot Jenny McCarthy's advice.

"I'd like my wife on top of me eating doughnuts."

Jonathan Ross reveals his inner Homer.

"Shane was a bit porky. At times it was like a bus was trying to have sex with me."

Porn babe Kelly Cooke on big-boned spinner Warney

"You know you've hit rock bottom when you're taping *Eurotrash*. There's no such thing as an ironic wank, sadly."

Al Murray

"I've got a problem with breast-feeding. Whenever my friends' wives gave birth I'd be round all the time. I'd be like, 'Oh look at little Darren. Isn't he lovely? He's hungry, you know.' 'No, he's just been fed.' 'No, look, he's fucking starving.'

'No, seriously, he's just…' 'Look, just get your tits out or I'll kill it!'"

Frank Skinner

"I was at the hospital for a blood test and I was stopped dead in my tracks by a sign which said, 'Family Planning Advice. Use The Back Entrance.'"

Dave Spikey

"Henry was very powerful and noisy. It was a romantic expression of one man's feelings for a vacuum cleaner."

Russell Brand podcasts about sex with a Henry vacuum cleaner

"What do atheists scream when they come?"

Bill Hicks

"I was recently asked to judge Mr Gay UK. I said no problem at all: he's against nature and he's going to hell."

Jimmy Carr

"I was stood in the kitchen and my husband came in. I said, 'Let's have it off on the floor.'
  He said, 'Why?'
  I said, 'Because I need to time an egg.'"

Lily Savage

"I can't find a woman anywhere who will touch me with a shitty stick.
  Fair enough. It is a bit of an unusual request."

Andrew Lawrence

"Sex and sleep are my two favourite things. If I could do both at the same time, I'd be a happy man. I always envy my girlfriend that trick."

Ed Byrne

"A woman walks into a pharmacy and asks if they sell extra-large condoms.
'Yes madam,' says the chemist.
'Would you like to know how much they are?'
'No thanks,' she says, 'but do you mind if I stand here and wait to see if anyone buys one?'"

"Sex is like bridge. If you don't have a good partner, you'd better have a good hand."

Woody Allen

'My grandad said, 'The problem with you lot, you think you invented sex!'
'Okay, Grandad,' I said, 'have you ever fucked Nana up the arse, pulled out and come on her tits?'
Turns out he had. That's what killed her."

Jimmy Carr.

"I listen well to women, I'm very considerate. And I encourage them to show their feelings. Because, apparently, that's the best way to let you fuck them."

Reginald D Hunter

"How do you get a fat girl into bed?"

Piece of cake.

"There's this campaign, 'If you're having sex tonight, make sure you get consent.' What sort of society is this if we have to remind people not to rape? 'I'm going out tonight, few pints, some rape.' 'You can't rape. It's illegal. Saw it on telly.' 'What? You mean you're not allowed to rape?'"

Ricky Gervais

"I was there in the delivery room, I saw what happened. Now anything my wife wants, gets done. She's like, 'Change the diaper,' and I'm like, 'Absolutely, sorry about your vagina.'"

Adam Sandler on owing his wife for the pain of childbirth.

"At what stage do you get embarrassed about 'enlarge your penis' emails? I'm not the only one getting them, am I? It's just currently I'm getting about ten a day. Eight of them are from my girlfriend. It's the two from my mum that really hurt.

Jimmy Carr

"For Christmas, my mates clubbed together and bought me a sweater. I'd have preferred a moaner or a screamer."

Tam Cowan

"The only thing I like about myself is my huge willy."

Robbie Williams: massive dick.

"I get plane-ons, cab-ons, limo-ons… My dick is hard all the time. I don't think it's normal."

Tommy Lee on his non-stop erection.

"I've got a friend who's fallen in love with two school bags. He's bisatchel."

Tim Vine

"After serving only three days of her prison sentence, Paris Hilton has been let out of jail. When asked about it, Paris said, 'Usually I'm not a fan of premature release.'"

Conan O'Brien

"Ladies aren't throwing themselves at me enough. For the record, if any women see me on the street and assume I've only got one thing on my mind, they're probably right."

Stephen Merchant laments his lack of female groupies

"The prison as scared Paris would go on hunger strike so they took all the porridge and flavoured it with sperm. She gained four pounds. But at one point, she went 'Ahh nooo, this has got porridge in it?'"

Frankie Boyle, 8 Out Of 10 Cats

"I'd kiss the mole on Amy Winehouse's face and every tattoo on her body. And I'd stick my tongue in the gap where her tooth is missing. I love her."

David Gest on what he'd do if he were invisible for the day

"I read in a magazine that 68% of British men masturbate on a regular basis. How do they know? Anyone I ask never does it. Did it show up on the Richter scale?"

Billy Connolly

"A bloke goes to the doctor with bad headaches. The doctor says, 'Can I ask you a personal question? Do you masturbate?' He says, 'Sometimes.' Doctor goes, ' Magic, ain't it.'"

Peter Kay.

"I recently filled in a questionnaire that asked me who I'd like to sleep with, anyone living or dead? I put 'anyone living.'"

Jimmy Carr

What do you call a lesbian with big fingers?
Hung.

"Borat was fine. There's nothing sexier than a big handlebar moustache. Call me crazy."

Sacha Baron Cohen's fiancée Isla Fisher

What do you say to a virgin when she sneezes?
Goes-in-tight!

My wife is a sex object – every time I ask for sex, she objects.

Why do women like orgasms?
So they can moan even when they're enjoying themselves.

What's the definition of trust?
Two cannibals giving each other a blowjob.

"Now we have gay bishops, official. I wonder if this will filter down into the game of chess? Bishops make all the same moves, but can only be taken from behind."

Jason Wood

"You know that look women get when they want sex? Me neither."

Peter Kay

What do you do if your girlfriend starts smoking?
Slow down and use some lubricant.

"If you're in a relationship and sex has got boring, try bondage. Get your lover, blindfold them, get some rope and chains, tie them to the bed or radiator, then go out and fuck someone else."

Stewart Lee

"I had hassle getting out tonight – I had to organise a baby sitter. I don't have children, I just find they're a lot cheaper than escorts."

Jimmy Carr

"I replaced the headlights in my car with strobe lights, so it looks like I'm the only one moving."

Steven Wright

"I know why they like me – I look good in or out of my top and I have a huge widger."

Gordon Ramsay on his gay fans

"Are there any women here who don't like giving blowjobs? I can't understand that. I had a woman at my last show go, 'Yeah, well have you ever tried it?' I said, 'Yeah. Almost broke my back.'"

Bill Hicks

"My sons love my stripper pole. They use it more than me."

Pamela Anderson must be very proud of Brandon, nine, and Dylan, eight

A man visits the doctor's because he has a severe stuttering problem. After a thorough examination, the doctor consults with the patient.

Doctor: "It appears that the reason for your stuttering is that your penis is about six inches too long and it is thus pulling on your vocal cords, and thereby causing you this annoying problem of stuttering."

"Ddddd octttor. Whhaaat cccan I dddo?"

The doctor scratches his forehead, thinks for a minute and states that there is a procedure where we can free up the strain on the vocal cords by removing the six inches from the penis and freeing him from this horrible problem. The patient stuttering badly states that this problem has caused him so much embarrassment as well as loss of employment that anything would be worth it. The doctor plans for the procedure. The operation is a success and six months later the patient comes in for his check up.

The patient says to the: "Doctor, the operation was a success. I have not stuttered since the operation. I have a great job and my self esteem is fantastic. However, there is one problem, my wife says that she sort of misses the great sex we used to have before the extra six inches were removed. So I was wondering if it is possible to reattach those six inches."

The doctor scratches his forehead, thinks for a minute and says: "I dddoonnnbt ttthhhinkkkk thatttt wooould bbbbee posssssssibbbble!"

"Watching sex on telly with Mum and Dad – that's embarrassing. I didn't even know they had a camcorder."

Jimmy Carr

Gongs Given at the 2007 AVN porn Awards

1. Best Anal-Themed Release- *Weapons of Ass Destruction 4* (Jules Jordan Video)
2. Best Interracial Series – *My Hot Wife Is Fucking Blackzilla* (Hush Hush Entertainment/Digital Sin)
3. Best Transsexual Series – *Transsexual Prostitutes* (Devil's Film)

4. Best Foreign Feature – *Porn Wars: Episode 1* (Private U.S.A. / Pure Play Media)

5. Best Specialty Release – *Fem-Dom Strap-On – Strap Attack 4* (Joey Silvera/Evil Angel)

6. Best Specialty Release – *Squirting – Flower's Squirt Shower 3* (Elegant Angel Productions)

7. Best Amateur Release- *Bang Bus 9* (Bang Productions)

8. Best Anal-Themed Series- *Big Wet Asses* (Elegant Angel Productions

9. Best Hard-Edged All-Sex Release – *Slave Dolls 2* (Elegant Angel)

10. Best Group Sex Scene – Video – *Fashionistas Safado: The Challenge* (Evil Angel Productions), Belladonna, Melissa Lauren, Jenna Haze, Gianna, Sandra Romain, Adrianna Nicole, Flower Tucci, Sasha Grey, Nicole Sheridan, Marie Luv, Caroline Pierce, Lea Baren, Jewell Marceau, Jean Val Jean, Christian XXX, Voodoo, Chris Charming, Erik Everhard, Mr. Pete, Rocco Siffredi

"Sure, I shave down there. I do it myself or I have my young lady help me, because I don't want to get no nicks."

Sean 'Diddy' Combs on his "downstairs" grooming.

A divorced man bumps into his ex-wife's new husband at a party. After knocking back a few drinks, he walks over to the guy and sneers: "So, how do you like using second-hand goods?" "Doesn't bother me," he replies. "Once you get past the first three inches, it's all brand new."

"Sex education at my school was a muttered warning about the janitor."

Frankie Boyle

"When a guy comes, he comes 200 million sperm. I've wiped entire civilisations of my chest with a grey gym sock."

Bill Hicks

So well-heeled pupils are in hot water after they were caught having sex on the playing field at posh public school Rugby. The stunned principal says he's never seen anything like it. Apparently, one of them was a girl.

Sex In Numbers

1 in 7 priests and nuns break their vows of chastity.

14% of males did not enjoy sex the first time, compared to 60% of women.

10.6 inches is the size of world's longest surgically-augmented penis, according to *The Guinness Book of Records*.

80% of men admit to climaxing while dreaming about sex, double the figure for women.

138 is the number of average shags a year for the Greeks, topping the global figures. They're followed by Croatians (134). Japanese are the least active on just 45 per year.

28mph is the speed of average man's initial spurt of ejaculate – faster than the world 100-metre sprint record.

1% of the adult female population is able to achieve orgasm solely through breast stimulation.

3 in 10 women over the age of 80 still have sexual intercourse.

112 calories are burned by the average female orgasm. A faked orgasm burns 315.

200 million couples around the world have sex per day – or about 2,000 shags happening at any given moment.

In the Aztec culture, avocados were considered so sexually powerful, virgins were restricted from contact with them.

Ecouteurism is listening to others having sex without their consent.

According to a recent survey, more Americans lose their virginity in June than any other month.

Hybristophilia is the arousal derived by having sex with criminals.

In America for three years during the 1950's, a campaign against 'naked animals' attracted considerable public support. Until, that is, the founders of the movement, Mr Trout and Mr Able, were exposed as inspired hoaxers.

In Pompeii, prostitutes had to dye their hair blue, red or yellow.

An analysis of speed-dating sessions across Britain found that every inch (2.5cm) a man has over a rival in height boosts his appeal to women by 5%.

Worldwide averages show that Jews and atheists have more sex partners than Catholics or Protestants.

Impotence is grounds for divorce in 26 US states.

As a tranquilizer in the world, sex is 10 times more effective than valium.

Besides the genitals and the breasts, the inner nose is the only other body part that swells during intercourse.

Australia has the planet's highest use of vibrators per head of population.

According to *Playboy*, more women talk dirty during sex than men.

Until 1972 in the US, homosexuality was officially a mental illness, classified with schizophrenia.

For every 35 pounds of weight a man carries over his ideal weight, his penis will appear to be one inch smaller.

In Florida and Washington DC, only the missionary position is legal.

The Romans would crush a first-time rapist's gonads between two stones.

Women with a PhD are TWICE as likely to be up for a one-night stand than those with a regular degree.

On Pacific island Guam, it is forbidden for virgins to marry, so there are men in Guam whose full-time job is to travel the country and deflower young women.

It takes a sperm one hour to swim seven inches.

If straight women had to choose a same-sex partner, a 2006 survey found that the most popular celebrity choice would by Davina McCall, followed by Jennifer Aniston and Kylie. Angelina Jolie surprisingly only collected 9% of the vote, lower than Zoe Ball.

Japan leads the world in condom use. Like cosmetics, they're sold door to door, by women.

The word pornography comes from the Greek meaning the "writings of prostitutes".

Of people who die suddenly during sex, eight in ten are in the act of cheating on their spouses

Men are most likely to have affairs in the month of December, while women prefer July.

There is a town in Canada called Dildo.

The most common place for adults to have sex outside the bedroom is in the car, followed by toilets and the park.

The word 'vanilla' comes from the Latin word vagina, because of the pod's resemblance to the female genitalia.

A man's testicles can increase in size by 50 per cent when he is aroused.

Adam came first.
But then, men always do.

Q. What's an Australian kiss?
A. The same as a French kiss, but Down Under.

Five Need-to-know Nuggets About Pornography

1. The Thais use pornography more than any other country.
2. 40% of British men in the UK admitted to using pornographic websites in 2006.
3. Women are the fastest-growing users of pornography on the internet.
4. Each year, in Los Angeles alone, more than 10,000 hardcore pornographic films are made, against an annual Hollywood average of just 400 movies.
5. Porn revenue is bigger than all combined revenues of all the professional football, baseball, and basketball franchises.

A man and a woman are having sex.
The woman says, "You haven't got AIDS, have you?"
He says no.
She says, "Thank God. I don't want to catch that again."

Semen is the most common body fluid found in hotel rooms.

An elderly couple go to bed together for the first time.
The old woman says, "Before we start, I have to warn you that I have acute angina."
The old man looks her up and down and says, "Yes, and your tits aren't bad either."

Q. Why are bankers good in bed?
A. They know the penalty for early withdrawal.

A bloke walking down the street sees a woman with perfect breasts.

He says, "Hey, would you let me bite your breasts for £100?"

She says, "Are you mad?"

He says, "OK, would you let me bite your breasts for £1,000?"

She says, "I'm not that kind of woman! Got it?"

He says, "OK, would you let me bite your breasts just once for £10,000?"

She thinks about it and says, "OK, just once, but not here. Let's go to that dark alley over there."

So they go into the alley, where she takes off her blouse to reveal the most perfect breasts in the world.

As soon as he sees them, he grabs them and starts caressing them, fondling them slowly, kissing them, licking them, burying his face in them – but not biting them.

The woman eventually gets annoyed and says, "Well? Are you going to bite them or not?"

"Nah," he says. "Costs too much."

A mother is cleaning her 12-year-old son's bedroom when she finds a series of bondage and fetish mags.

She shouts for her husband to come and see.

She yells, "What the hell am I supposed to do about this lot?"

The father says, "I don't know, but whatever you do, don't spank him."

Q. What does a bull do to stay warm on a cold day?
A. He slips into a nice warm Jersey.

Q. What did Cinderella do when she got to the ball?
A. Gag.

A man in a pub asks for a pint.
The barman says, "Sure, that'll be a penny."
"A penny?" exclaims the man. Reading the menu, he says, "Could I have steak and chips?"
"Certainly," says the barman, "that'll be fourpence."
"Four pence?" cries the man. "You're joking. Where's the bloke who owns this place?"
The barman says, "Upstairs, with my wife."
The man says, "What's he doing upstairs with your wife?"
The barman says, "The same thing I'm doing to his business."

Q. Why don't women blink during foreplay?
A. They don't have time.

Q. What do a bungee jump and a prostitute have in common?
A. They're cheap, fast and if the rubber breaks, you're dead.

A cheating wife is having sex with her lover when the phone rings. She picks it up, listens for a couple of minutes, puts it down and says, "That was my husband."

Worried, her lover starts to put his clothes on.

"Calm down," she says, "we've got plenty of time. He's playing cards with you and the rest of his mates."

Q. What do a clitoris, a woman's birthday and a toilet have in common?
A. Men always miss them.

A cowboy is riding on the plains.

He comes across a Red Indian boy lying naked on his back with a huge erection.

The cowboy says, "What the hell are you doing?'"

The Indian takes a look at the shadow of his cock and says, "It's 1pm."

The cowboy rides on.

Soon he runs into another Red Indian. He too is lying on his back naked with a huge erection.

The cowboy says, "What the hell are you doing?"

The Indian looks at the shadow of his cock and says, "It's 2.30pm."

The cowboy rides on.

Later he comes upon a third Red Indian. This one is lying on his back naked, masturbating.

The cowboy says, "Christ! What the hell are you doing?'"

The Indian says, "I'm winding my watch."

Q. Why is a man's urine yellow and his sperm white?
A. So he can tell if he's coming or going.

Q. What have a bungee jump and a blow-job from an 80-year-old got in common?
A. They're great if you don't look down.

Some nurses are bathing a woman in a coma when one of them notices a slight response on the monitor when they touch her genitals.

So they go to her husband and say, "Crazy as this sounds, maybe a little oral sex will bring her out of the coma."

The husband is sceptical, but they assure him that with the curtains closed for privacy it might just work. He finally agrees and goes into his wife's room.

A few minutes pass and then the woman's monitor flat-lines and the alarm starts ringing. The nurses burst into the room.

"What happened?" they cry.

The husband says, "I think she choked."

A guy goes to a disco, picks up a Chinese woman and takes her home.

She says, "I'll do anything you want."

He says, "How about a 69?"

She says, "I'm not cooking at this time of night."

Two lovers go to the mountains for a winter break and the man goes out to chop wood.

When he gets back, he says to his girlfriend, "My hands are freezing."

She says, "Well, put them between my legs to warm up."

He does, and it works.

After lunch, he goes back out to chop more wood, comes back and says again, "My hands are freezing."

Again she says, "Put them between my legs."

He does, and again it works.

After dinner, he goes to chop wood for the night. When he returns, he says, "Darling, my hands are freezing!"

She looks at him and says, "For crying out loud, don't your ears ever get cold?"

Q. Why do women close their eyes during sex?

A. Because they can't stand to see a man having a good time.

A virgin couple are on their honeymoon. Before they have sex, the wife says she has something to confess.

The husband says, "I will love you no matter what it is. Tell me."

The wife tells him that she is extremely flat-chested.

The husband takes off her shirt and says, "Yes, you are small, but I love you anyway. Now, I have something to confess too."

She says, "I will love you no matter what it is. Just tell me."

He says, "OK. I'm built like a baby down there."

She says, "I can deal with that."

So he pulls down his pants and his wife passes out. He fans her and she finally gets up.

She says, "I thought you said you were built like a baby?"

He says, "Yes: 7lbs, 21 inches."

A couple start having sex in the middle of a dark forest.

After about 15 minutes, the man gets up and says, "Damn, I wish I had a torch."

The woman says, "Me too – you've been eating grass for the last 10 minutes."

A woman tells her doctor that she's got bad carpet burns on her knees.

The doctor asks how she got them and she tells him it's from having sex doggy-style.

The doctor bandages her knees.

She says, "What can I do to avoid this?"

He says, "Couldn't you try having sex in different positions?"

She says, "That's OK for me, but what about the dog?"

Q. What do you do if your boiler explodes?

A. Buy her some flowers.

A doctor has a great reputation for helping couples improve their sex life, but always promises not to take a case if he feels he can't help them.

The Browns come to see the doctor, and he gives them thorough physical examinations. He concludes, "Yes, I'm happy to say that I can help you. On your way home from my surgery, stop at the supermarket and buy some grapes and some doughnuts. Go home, take off your clothes, and you, sir, roll the grapes across the floor until you make a bullseye in your wife's crotch. Then, on hands and knees, you must crawl to her like a leopard and retrieve the grape using only your tongue."

He adds, "Ma'am, you must take the doughnuts and, from across the room, toss them at your husband until you make a ringer around his penis. Then, like a lioness, you must crawl to him and eat the doughnut, using only your lips."

The couple go home and their sex life becomes more and more wonderful.

They tell their friends, the Greens, that they should see the doctor.

The doctor tells the Greens he won't take the case unless he feels he can help them. So he conducts the same physical examinations.

Then he tells the Greens the bad news. "I can't help you. I believe your sex life is as good as it will ever be."

The Greens plead with him, and say, "You helped our friends the Browns" now please help us."

The doctor says, "Oh, all right. On your way home, stop at the supermarket and buy some apples and a box of Cheerios…"

A bloke gets back from the doctor's one day and tells his wife he's only got 24 hours to live.

Wiping away her tears, he asks her to have sex with him. Of course, she agrees, and they make passionate love.

Six hours later, he says, "Darling, now I have only 18 hours to live. Can we have sex again?"

She agrees.

Later, he's getting into bed when he realises he now has only eight hours of life left.

He says, "Darling? Please? Just one more time before I die."

She agrees; then afterwards she rolls over and falls asleep.

He, however, hears the clock ticking, and he tosses and turns until he's down to only four more hours. He taps his wife on the shoulder to wake her up.

He says, "Darling, I only have four hours left. Could we…?"

His wife sits up abruptly and yells, "Look, I have to get up in the morning – you don't."

What are the three worst things about being an egg?
You only get laid once, it takes ten minutes to go hard and the only bird to sit on your face is your mum.

Q. Why do woman fake orgasms?
A. Because they think men care.

Q. What have a fat woman and a moped got in common?
A. They're both OK for a ride until your mates find out.

A woman on her death bed calls her husband and instructs him to look under their bed and open the wooden box he finds.

He's puzzled by the three eggs and £7,000 in cash he finds inside, so he asks his wife what the eggs are for.

"Oh, those?" she says. "Every time we had bad sex, I put an egg in the box."

Not bad after 35 years of marriage, thinks the husband.

Then he says, "But what about the £7,000?"

"Oh, that?" she says. "Every time I got a dozen I sold them."

Q. Why is it that it's mainly female sperm that find the egg first?
A. Male sperm won't stop and ask for directions.

Two gay men are having sex when the phone starts to ring.

One of them rises to answer it and says, "I'll be just a minute. Don't finish yourself off until I get back."

The second bloke says, "OK."

A few minutes later, the first bloke comes back into the room and sees semen everywhere.

The first bloke says, "I told you to wait till I got back before you finished."

The second bloke says, "I didn't; I just farted."

Q. How can you tell who's the head nurse?
A. She's the one with the dirty knees.

A bloke is suffering from severe headaches.

The doctor says, "I suffered from that type of headache for years, too. This is how I cured it. Every day I'd give my wife oral sex. When she came, she'd squeeze her legs together with all her strength, and the pressure would relieve the tension in my head. Try that every day for two weeks, then come back and let me know how it goes."

Two weeks go by and the man is back.

He says, "Doctor, I feel great. I haven't had a headache since I started this treatment. I can't thank you enough."

The doctor says, "Glad to hear it."

The man says, "Thanks. And by the way, you have a lovely home."

Q. What goes in hard and pink, but comes out soft and mushy?
A. Bubblegum.

Q. What's the difference between love and herpes?
A. Love doesn't last for ever.

Q. What do you get if you cross a Mac with a nun?
A. A computer that will never go down on you.

A heart surgeon dies and is given an elaborate funeral. An enormous heart covered in flowers stands behind the casket during the service.

Following the eulogy, the heart opens, and the casket rolls inside.

The heart then closes, sealing the surgeon inside the beautiful heart for ever.

At that point, one of the mourners bursts into laughter. Everyone stares at him.

He says, "I'm sorry; I was just thinking of my own funeral. I'm a gynaecologist."

That's when the rectal surgeon fainted.

A jelly baby goes to the doctor and asks if he can have an AIDS test.
The doctor says, "Why? What the hell have you been up to?"
The jelly baby says, "Fucking allsorts."

A German visits a prostitute and says, "I vish to buy sex vit you. I must varn you: I am a little kinky."

The prostitute says, "No problem."

So off they go to the prostitute's flat, where the German produces four large bedsprings and a duck call.

He says, "I vant you to tie ze springs to each of your limbs."

The prostitute finds this odd, but complies, fastening the springs to her hands and knees.

He says, "Now you vill get on your hans und knees."

She obeys, balancing on the springs.

He says, "You vill please blow zis vistle as I make love to you."

She thinks this weird but it seems harmless and after all, the German is paying.

The sex is fantastic. She is bounced all over the room by the energetic German, all the time honking on the duck call.

The climax is the most sensational that she has ever experienced, and it's several minutes before she's recovered her breath sufficiently to say, "That was amazing. What do you call that?"

The German says, "Four sprung duck technique."

Q. What did the leper say to the prostitute?
A. "Keep the tip."

A man goes into a chemist and asks if they've got any KY jelly.

The woman behind the counter says, "Sorry, we haven't. Have you tried Boots?"

The man says, "I want to slide in, not march in."

Q. Why do women have two holes so close together?
A. In case you miss.

Q. How many mice does it take to screw in a light-bulb?
A. Two, if they're small enough.

Ethel is a demon in her wheelchair, and loves to charge around the nursing home, taking corners on one wheel and getting up to maximum speed on the long corridors.

Because the poor woman is one sandwich short of a picnic, the other residents tolerate her, and some of the blokes even join in.

One day, Ethel is speeding up the corridor when a door opens and Mad Clarence steps forward with his arm outstretched.

"Stop!" he shouts. "Have you got a licence for that thing?"

Ethel fishes around in her handbag, pulls out a Kit Kat wrapper and holds it up to him.

"OK," he says, and Ethel speeds off down the hall.

As she takes the corner near the TV lounge on one wheel, Weird Harold pops out in front of her and shouts, "Stop! Have you got proof of insurance?"

Ethel digs into her handbag, pulls out a beermat and holds it up to him.

Harold nods and says, "Carry on, ma'am."

As Ethel nears the final corridor before the front door, Crazy Craig steps out in front of her, stark naked, with a huge erection in his hand.

"Oh, good grief," says Ethel, "not the breathalyser again."

Q. What do the Mafia and cunnilingus have in common?

A. One slip of the tongue and you're in deep shit.

Q. Why can't Miss Piggy count to 70?
A. She gets a frog in her throat at 69.

Q. What do you get if you cross a pitbull with a prostitute?
A. Your last blow-job.

A little girl goes to see Santa.
Santa says, "What would you like Santa to bring you for Christmas?"
She says, "I want a Barbie and Action Man."
Santa says, "I thought Barbie came with Ken."
She says, "No: she comes with Action Man; she fakes it with Ken."

A man is out shopping and discovers a new brand of condoms – Olympic.

He buys a pack, then tells his wife.

She says, "Olympic condoms? What makes them so special?"

He says, "There are three colours: gold, silver and bronze."

She says, "What colour are you going to wear tonight?"

He says, "Gold, of course!"

She says, "Can't you wear silver? It would be nice if you didn't come first for once."

The year is 2222 and Mike and Maureen land on Mars after accumulating enough frequent flier miles.

They meet a Martian couple and have a chat. Maureen brings up the subject of sex.

She says, "Just how do you guys do it?"

The Martian says, "Pretty much the way you do."

The couples decide to swap partners for the night to see what it's like.

Maureen and the male Martian go off to a bedroom where the Martian strips. He's got a tiny penis – half an inch long and a quarter of an inch thick.

Maureen says, "I don't think this is going to work. It's just not long enough."

The Martian says, "No problem," and proceeds to slap his forehead with his palm. With each slap of his forehead, his penis grows until it's impressively long.

She says, "That's great, but it's still pretty thin."

The Martian says, "No problem," and starts pulling his ears. With each pull, his penis grows thicker and thicker until it's huge.

"Wow!" she says, as they fall into bed and have passionate sex.

The next day the couples rejoin their normal partners and go their separate ways.

Mike says, "Well, was it any good?"

Maureen says, "I hate to say it, but it was wonderful. How about you?"'

He says, "It was horrible. All I got was a headache – she kept slapping my forehead and pulling my ears."

Did you hear about the nymphomaniac parrot?
 She liked a cock or two.

A bloke goes to his optometrist to have his eyes examined.
 The optometrist says, "Joe, you've got to stop masturbating!"
 Joe says, "Why, Doc? Am I going blind?"
 The optometrist says, "No, but you're upsetting my other patients."

Two nuns are in the bath.
 One nun says to the other, "Where's the soap?"
 The other says, "Yes, it does, doesn't it?"

A man emerges from the bathroom naked and climbs into bed in the mood for sex, but, as usual, his wife says, "I have a headache."
 "Don't worry," he says. "I was just in the bathroom powdering my cock with aspirin. You can take it orally or as a suppository: it's up to you."

Q. What's the difference between oral sex and anal sex?
A. Oral sex makes your day, anal sex makes your hole weak.

Q. What do you call a prostitute with a runny nose?
A. Full.

A man and his wife go on a second honeymoon for their 25th anniversary.

At the hotel, the woman says, "When you first saw my naked body, what was going through your mind?"

The man says, "All I wanted to do was to fuck your brains out and suck your tits dry."

Then, as the wife seductively undresses, she says, "What are you thinking now?"

He says, "It looks as if I did a pretty good job."

Q. When is a pixie not a pixie?

A. When he's got his head up a fairy's skirt – then he's a goblin.

A paper bag goes to the doctors and says, "There's something wrong with my privates."

The doctor has a look and says, "I'm sorry to say you have AIDS."

The paper bag says, "How? I'm a virgin – I've never had sex."

The doctor says, "Your mum must be a carrier."

A young boy says, "Mum, is it true people come apart like machines?"

"Of course not, darling," she replies, "what gave you that idea?"

"Well," the boy says, "I overheard Daddy on the phone saying he was screwing the arse off his secretary."

A bloke has a new job in a pickle factory.

For weeks, he has a strange urge to stick his dick into the pickle slicer.

He finally comes clean to his wife, who begs him not to do it.

But he can't control himself, and his urge grows greater and greater.

One day he comes home from work, and tells his wife that he's done it.

"My God!" says his wife, "what happened?"

"I got fired," says the bloke.

"No," says his wife, "I mean, what happened about the pickle slicer?"

"Oh," says the bloke, "she got fired too."

Q. How do you know if a public schoolboy is a gentlemen?
A. He'll take a girl out five times before shagging her younger brother.

Two old men are comparing their libidos.

The first one says, "I can still do it twice."

The other says, "Which time do you prefer?"

The first one says, "Usually the winter."

They've invented the most realistic vibrator yet. Just before she orgasms, the vibrator comes, goes limp, farts and switches itself off.

A man comes home one night, and his wife throws her arms around his neck and cries, "Darling, I have great news: I'm a month overdue. I think we're going to have a baby! The doctor gave me a test today, but until we find out for sure, we can't tell anybody."

The next day, a bloke from the electric company rings the doorbell, because the couple haven't paid their last bill.

He says, "Are you Mrs Smith? You're a month overdue."

"How did you know?" stammers the young woman.

"It's in our files," says the man.

"What? Well, let me talk to my husband about this tonight."

That night, she tells her husband about the visit, and he, mad as a bull, rushes to the electric company's office first thing the next morning.

He yells, "What's going on? You have it on file that my wife is a month overdue? What business is that of yours?"

"Just calm down," says the bloke, "it's nothing serious. All you have to do is pay us."

"Pay you? And if I refuse?"

"In that case, sir, we'd have no option but to cut yours off."

"And what would my wife do then?"

"I don't know. I suppose she'd have to use a candle."

A man is lying naked on a beach when a sexy girl comes over and starts slapping his arse rhythmically.
He says, "What are you doing?"
She says, "Playing the bongos."
He turns over and says, "Can you play the flute?"

A woman goes to her therapist and moans, "Every time we're in bed and my husband has an orgasm, he lets out an ear-splitting yell."

The therapist says, "That's completely natural. I don't see what the problem is."

She says, "It wakes me up."

An 18-year-old girl tells her mother she's missed her period for two months.

Worried, the mother buys a pregnancy test kit. The result shows that the girl is pregnant.

Furious, the mother yells, "Who was the pig that did this to you?"

The girl picks up the phone and makes a call.

Half an hour later a Ferrari stops outside.

A man in a very expensive suit climbs out and enters the house.

He sits in the living room with the father, the mother and the girl, and says, "Your daughter has informed me of the problem. I can't marry her because of my family situation, but I'll take charge. If a girl is born, I will bequeath her two shops, a townhouse, a beach villa and a £1,000,000 bank account. If a boy is born, my legacy will be a couple of factories and a £2,000,000 bank account. If it's twins, a factory and £1,000,000 each. However, if there is a miscarriage, what do you suggest I do?"

The father places a hand firmly on the man's shoulder and says, "Fuck her again."

For Christmas, my wife asked for something long, thin and hard with a rubber on the end.

So I brought her the finest pencil money could buy.

For her birthday, she asked for something around six inches with a head on it.

So I gave her a tenner.

An 85-year-old man goes to his doctor to get a sperm count.

The doctor gives the man a jar and says, "Take this jar home and bring back a semen sample tomorrow."

The next day the old man reappears at the surgery and gives him the jar, which is still empty. The doctor asks what went wrong.

The old man says, "First I tried with my right hand, but nothing. Then I tried with my left hand, but still nothing. Then I asked my wife for help. She tried with her right hand, then her left, still nothing. She tried with her mouth, and still nothing. We even called up the lady next door and she tried too: first with both hands, then an armpit, and she even tried squeezing it between her knees. But still nothing."

Shocked, the doctor says, "You asked your neighbour?"

The old man says, "Yes. And no matter what we tried, we still couldn't get the jar open."

Q. What do a Rubik's Cube and a penis have in common?
A. The longer you play with them, the harder they get.

Q. How do men practise safe sex?
A. They meet their bit on the side at least 10 miles from where they live.

Q. What is a man's definition of safe sex?
A. A padded headboard.

Q. How do you get a nun pregnant?
A. Dress her up as an altar boy.

A man wearing a mask bursts into a sperm bank holding a shotgun.

"Open the safe!" he yells at the woman behind the counter.

"But we're not a real bank," she says. "This is a sperm bank: we don't hold money."

He says, "Don't argue – just open the safe or I'll blow your head off."

She obliges and opens the safe door.

He says, "Take one of the bottles and drink it."

She says, "But it's full of sperm."

He says, "Don't argue; just drink it."

She takes off the cap and gulps it down.

He says, "Take out another bottle and drink it too."

The girl drinks another one.

Suddenly the bloke pulls off the mask and, to the woman's amazement, it's her husband.

He says, "See? Not that bloody difficult, is it?"

Q. Why are men so bad at sex and driving?
A. Because they always pull out with no thought of who else might be coming.

A Scottish woman walks in on her husband wanking into a welly. She yells, "Stop fucking aboot!"

A married redneck couple are sitting on the couch watching the news on TV in Alabama.

The man says, "Look at them homosexuals demanding the right to be married. They're ruining the sanctity of our institution. We oughta go to San Francisco just to show those liberals that marriage means one man, one woman. Right, darling?"

The woman says, "Right, Daddy!"

Q. What do you call a man who expects to have sex on the second date?
A. Slow.

Q. Why do men masturbate?
A. It's sex with someone they love.

Q. What bees make milk?
A. Boo-bees.

Big Gay Glenn goes to the doctor and has some tests. The doctor comes back and says, "Glenn, I'm not going to beat about the bush. You have AIDS."

Glenn is devastated. "Doctor, what can I do?"

"Eat one sausage, one head of cabbage, 20 unpeeled carrots drenched in hot sauce, 10 Jalapeno peppers, 40 walnuts, 40 peanuts, half a box of Grape Nuts, and top it off with a gallon of prune juice."

Glenn asks, "Will that cure me, Doctor?"

The doctor says, "No, but it should leave you with a better understanding of what your arse is for."

A bloke is very ashamed because he has an extremely small penis and doesn't want his girlfriend to dump him when she sees its size.

One night when he and his girlfriend are snogging in a dark corner he decides to show her. The man unzips his trousers, whips out his tiny penis and shoves it in her hand.

She says, "Thanks, but I don't smoke."

Q. What do Brussels sprouts and a woman's pubic hair have in common?

A. You push them aside and carry on eating.

Q. What do you call a woman with her tongue sticking out?

A. A lesbian with a hard-on.

Q. What's the difference between a woman and a fridge?
A. A fridge doesn't fart when you pull your meat out.

Q. What do women and police cars have in common?
A. They both make a lot of noise to let you know they're coming.

Two sperm are swimming side by side. One turns to the other and asks, "How much further to go?" The other says, "Bloody miles – we're only just past the tonsils."

A bloke walks into a chemist and says to the assistant, "I have three girls coming over tonight. I've never had three at once, so I need something to keep me horny."

The chemist gives him a box of mysterious pills marked with an 'X' and says, "Here, if you eat these you'll be rock-hard for 12 hours."

The bloke says, "Brilliant! Give me three boxes.'"

The next day, the bloke walks into the same chemist and pulls down his trousers. The assistant looks in horror as he notices the man's cock is black and blue, with skin hanging off in places.

The man says, "Give me a tube of Deep Heat."

The assistant says, "Deep Heat? You're not going to put Deep Heat on that, are you?"

The man says, "No, it's for my arms – the girls didn't show up."

Q. How can you tell if a man's sexually aroused?
A. He's breathing.

Mr Smith has two employees, Sarah and Jack.

They're both extremely good workers. However, Mr Smith looks over his books one day and decides that he isn't making enough money to warrant two employees, and he'll have to make one redundant.

But he has trouble finding a fair way to do it. He decides to watch them work, and the first one to take a break will be the one he lays off.

So he sits in his office and watches them. Suddenly, Sarah gets a headache and needs to take an aspirin. She takes the aspirin out of her purse and goes to the water cooler to get a drink to wash it down.

Mr Smith follows her to the water cooler, taps her on the shoulder and says, "Sarah, I'm going to have to lay you or Jack off."

Sarah says, "I have a headache – can you jack off?"

Q. What did the man say to the toothpaste model after she gave him a blow-job?

A. 'Those are the whitest teeth I've ever come across.'

Have you heard about the new super-sensitive condoms?
They hang around after the man leaves and talk to the woman.

A cruise in the Pacific goes wrong, the ship sinks and there are only three survivors: Damian, Darren and Deirdre.

They manage to swim to a small island, and they live there, doing what's natural for men and women to do.

After a couple of years, the previously chaste Deirdre feels so bad about having casual sex with two men that she kills herself.

It's a tragic time but Damian and Darren manage to get through it. They still have sexual needs, and so, after a while, nature once more takes its inevitable course.

But a couple more years later, Damian and Darren begin to feel ashamed of what they're doing.

So they bury her.

Q. What do you do if your girlfriend starts smoking?

A. Slow down and use some lubricant.

Little Johnny sees that his friend at school has a new watch, so he asks him how he got it.

His friend says, "I waited until I heard the bedsprings squeaking in my parents' bedroom and then I ran in. My father gave me a watch to get rid of me."

So Johnny goes home and waits until he hears the bedsprings squeaking and then runs into his parents' bedroom.

His father yells, "What's up?"

Johnny says, "I wanna watch!"

His father says, "Well, then, sit down and shut up!"

An American businessman has a meeting in France.

He meets a woman and that night they have a special kind of meeting of their own.

While they're having sex, she yells, "Trou faux, trou faux!" He doesn't know what that means, but assumes it to be some sort of praise.

The next day, he plays golf with the men from the meeting.

One of them hits a hole in one, so the businessman cries, "Trou faux, trou faux!"

The other man looks at him and says, "What do you mean, wrong hole?"

Two eggs are boiling in a saucepan. One says to the other, "Look, I've got a crack."

The other says, "No point telling me; I'm not hard yet."

An Italian, Frenchman and an Englishman are in the pub, chatting about their wives.

The Italian says, "I made love to my wife last night, and straight after I kissed her feet – she rose six inches off the bed."

The Frenchman says, "That's nothing. I made love to my wife last night, and straight after I licked the inside of her thighs – she rose 12 inches off the bed."

The English bloke says, "Oh, yeah? Well, I knobbed my missus last night, shot my bolt, wiped my cock on the curtains and she hit the roof!"

A guy falls asleep on the beach for several hours and gets horrible sunburn.

He goes to the hospital and is promptly admitted after being diagnosed with second-degree burns on his legs. He's starting to blister and he's in agony.

The doctor prescribes continuous intravenous feeding with saline and electrolytes, a sedative and, every four hours, a Viagra pill.

The nurse says, "What good will Viagra do him?"

The doctor says, "It'll keep the sheets off his legs."

An ugly man walks into his local wearing a big grin.

The landlord says, "What are you so happy about?"

The ugly man says, "Well, I live by the railway. On my way home last night, I saw a young woman tied to the tracks, like in the films. I cut her free and took her back to my place. To cut a long story short, I had sex with her all night, in every room in the house."

The landlord says, "Fantastic! You lucky bastard. Was she pretty?"

The ugly man says, "Dunno, I never found the head."

Q. What do a walrus and Tupperware have in common?

A. They both like a tight seal.

Dave is about to marry Davina and his father takes him to one side.

He says, "When I married your mother, the first thing I did when we got home was take off my trousers. I gave them to your mother and told her to put them on. When she did, they were enormous on her and she said to me that she couldn't possibly wear them. I said, 'Of course they're too big. I wear the trousers in this family and I always will.'" Ever since that day, we've never had a single problem."

Dave takes his father's advice, and as soon as he gets Davina alone after the wedding, he does the same thing: takes off his trousers, gives them to Davina and tells her to put them on.

Davina says the trousers are too big and that she couldn't possibly wear them. Dave says, "Exactly. I wear the trousers in this relationship and I always will. I don't want you to forget that."

Davina pauses, removes her knickers and gives them to Dave.

She says, "Try these on."

He does, but they're too small.

He says, "I can't possibly get into your knickers."

She says, "Exactly. And if you don't change your attitude, you never will."

Q. What's worse than your doctor telling you you've got VD?

A. Your dentist telling you you've got VD.

Q. What's the ultimate rejection?
A. Your hand falling asleep as you masturbate.

A young couple get married and, according to tradition in their families, the best man has the first dance with the bride.

But the couple continue to dance for the second song, too; then the third. By the time they get to the fourth, the groom rushes up and boots the bride between the legs.

There's a riot. Eventually all the guests are hauled off by the police to appear in court.

The judge asks the best man what happened.

"Your honour," says the best man, "we were just dancing, and the groom ran up and booted the bride between the legs."

"That must have hurt," says the judge.

"It certainly did," said the best man, "it broke three of my fingers!"

Two whales overturn a ship using their blowholes.

"Can we eat the crew?" asks one.

"No," says the other. "I do blow-jobs but I don't swallow seamen."

Q. What do you call an adolescent rabbit?
A. A pubic hare.

Q. How many babies does it take to paint a wall?
A. Depends how hard you throw them.

Q. What's brown and hides in the attic?
A. The diarrhoea of Anne Frank.

A coach of blind kids are on a day trip when the driver feels thirsty. He spots a pub and pulls up.

He says, "Time for a break. Here's a field – what would you like to do?"

One boy says they'd like to play football.

The driver says, "But you're blind. Are you able to play?"

The boy says, "Yes, we've got a special ball that has a bell in so we can follow it."

So the driver goes to the pub. A while later, a policeman bursts through the pub door and yells, "Who's in charge of those blind kids?"

The driver says, "They're not causing trouble, are they?"

The policeman says, "Trouble? They've just kicked a Morris dancer to death."

Q. Why did the baker have smelly hands?
A. He kneaded a crap.

Q. What's the biggest drawback in the jungle?
A. An elephant's foreskin.

A drunk is staggering down the street with his car keys in his hand and his cock hanging out when he sees a policeman.

He points at his keys and says, "Officer, somebody's stolen my car."

The policeman says, "Where did you last see it?"

The drunk says, "On the end of this key."

The policeman notices that the drunk's cock is hanging out and says, "Sir, are you aware that you're exposing yourself?"

The drunk looks down and cries, "Oh no, they got my girlfriend too!"

Q. What is blonde, brunette, blonde, brunette, blonde?
A. A blonde doing cartwheels.

X-RATED

Q. What's blue and orange and lies at the bottom of a swimming pool?
A. A baby with burst armbands.

A woman goes into a pet shop and decides to buy a parrot.

The assistant says, "I must warn you: this parrot used to live in a brothel." The woman is concerned, but decides to buy it anyway.

When the woman gets home, she leaves the parrot in the lounge and waits for the reaction from her family.

Her son comes into the room. The parrot says, "Who's a pretty boy, then?"

The woman thinks, "That's OK."

Then her daughter walks in. The parrot says, "Hello, sexy."

The woman thinks, "Well, that's not too bad. I shouldn't have worried."

Then her husband gets back from work. The parrot says, "Hi, John, not seen you since last week."

Q. How can you tell you're at a bulimic stag do?
A. The cake jumps out of the stripper.

Q. How do you circumcise a bloke from Norwich?
A. Kick his sister in the jaw.

Q. What did the cannibal do after he dumped his girlfriend?
A. Wiped his arse.

Q. What's worse than a cardboard box?
A. Paper tits.

A pregnant woman is walking down the street when she gets caught up in a bank robbery getaway and is shot three times in the stomach.

Miraculously, she makes a full recovery and gives birth to triplets: one boy and two girls.

One day, about 16 years later, one of the girls runs to the mother in tears.

The woman says, "What's the matter?"

The daughter sobs, "I went to the toilet and a bullet came out."

A couple of weeks later, the second girl runs in crying, after exactly the same thing has happened to her.

Another week later, the boy runs to his mother and, like his sisters, he's in tears.

His mother says, "Let me guess: you went to the toilet and a bullet came out?"

The boy says, "No, I was having a wank and I shot the dog!'"

Two paedophiles are on a beach. One says to the other, 'Can you get out of my son, please?'

A girl asks her boyfriend to come over on Friday night and have dinner with her parents, and says that after dinner, she'd like to have sex with him for the first time.

The boy is ecstatic, but he's never had sex before, so he goes to the chemist to get some condoms.

The chemist asks the boy how many condoms he'd like to buy: a three-pack, a six-pack or a 10-pack. The boy chooses the 10-pack because he reckons he'll be busy.

That night, the boy shows up at the girl's house and meets his girlfriend at the door.

She says, "Oh, I'm so excited that you're going to meet my parents. Come in!"

The boy goes inside and is taken to the dinner table, where the girl's parents are seated. The boy decides to say grace and bows his head.

Ten seconds passes, and the boy is still deep in prayer, with his head down.

Twenty seconds pass, and still no movement from the boy.

Finally, after the boy has spent a minute with his head down, his girlfriend leans over and whispers, "I had no idea you were this religious."

The boy whispers back, "I had no idea your dad was a chemist."

What's the difference between getting caught speeding and going down on a woman?
When you go down on a woman, you can see the twat behind the bush.

Q. What is the difference between a clever midget and a venereal disease?
A. One is a cunning runt…

Q. What goes, "Click… Is that it? Click… Is that it? Click… Is that it?"
A. A blind person with a Rubik's cube.

Q. How do you make a cat go woof?
A. Cover it in petrol and light a match.

Q. What do a dildo and soy beans have in common?
A. They're both used as meat substitutes.

Q. Why haven't scientists found a cure for AIDS?
A. They can't get the laboratory mice to do anal.

A man goes into a chemist and asks for some deodorant.
The assistant says, "Ball or aerosol?"
The man says, "Neither. It's for my armpits."

A bloke holds a party where his guests are asked to dress as different emotions.

The first guest arrives. The host opens the door to see a bloke covered in green paint with the letters 'N' and 'V' painted on his chest.

He says "What emotion have you come as?"

The bloke says, "I'm green with envy."

A few minutes later, the next guest arrives. The host opens the door to see a woman covered in a pink body stocking with a feather boa wrapped around her privates.

The host says, "What emotion are you?"

She says, "I'm tickled pink."

A couple of minutes later, the doorbell rings for the third time and the man opens the door to see two Irish blokes, Paddy and Mick, standing there stark naked, one with his cock in a bowl of custard and the other with his cock stuck in a pear.

Shocked, the host says, "What emotions are these supposed to be?"

Paddy says, "Well, I'm fucking discustard, and Mick has just come in despair."

A doctor's just finished a marathon shagging session with a patient when he gets a tinge of guilt.

He thinks, "It wasn't really ethical to screw one of my patients."

But a little voice in his head says, "Who cares? I bet lots of doctors do it."

That makes the doctor feel a bit better, until another little voice says, "But they probably aren't vets."

An elephant says to a camel, "Why are your boobs on your back?"

The camel says, "That's rich, coming from someone with a dick on his face."

Q. Why does a dog lick its penis?
A. Because it can't make a fist.

Q. What does a dwarf get when he runs through a woman's legs?
A. A clit round the ear and a flap across the face.

Q. Did you hear about the dyslexic pimp?
A. He opened a warehouse.

Did you hear about the two gay blokes who had a row in a pub? They went outside to exchange blows.

Q. What's the difference between erotic and kinky?
A. Erotic is using a feather; kinky is using the whole chicken.

Q. What's the first sign of AIDS?
A. A pounding sensation in the arse.

Q. How can you tell if a Western is gay?
A. All the good guys are hung.

The teacher says, "Let's discuss what your dads do for a living."

Mary says, "My dad is a lawyer; He puts bad guys in jail."

Jack says, "My dad is a doctor; He makes sick people better."

Johnny doesn't raise his hand, so the teacher says, "Johnny, what does your dad do?"

Johnny says, "My dad's dead."

The teacher says, "I'm sorry to hear that. But what did he do before he died?"

Johnny says, "He turned blue and shat on the carpet."

Q. How can you tell you're in a gay theme park?
A. They issue gerbils at the Tunnel of Love.

Q. What's green and yellow and eats nuts?
A. Gonorrhoea.

An Irishman has been drinking at a pub all night.

The landlord finally says that the bar is closing. But when the Irishman stands up to leave, he falls flat on his face. He tries to stand again, with the same result.

He decides to crawl outside and get some fresh air to sober him up.

Once outside, he tries to stand up – but again falls flat on his face. So he decides to crawl home. When he arrives at the door, he tries to stand up – but again falls flat on his face. He crawls through the door and into his bedroom.

When he reaches his bed, he tries once again to stand up. This time he manages to pull himself upright, but immediately he collapses on to the duvet and falls asleep.

He's awakened the next morning by his wife shouting, "So, you've been out drinking again!"

He says, "What makes you say that?"

She says, "The pub called – you left your wheelchair there again."

Did you hear about the new Exorcist film?

They get the Devil to come in to take the priest out of the child.

Q. What's grey, sits at the end of your bed and takes the piss?

A. A kidney dialysis machine.

Q. What's the difference between a G-spot and a golf ball?

A. A man will actually search for a golf ball.

Q. What do a short-sighted gynaecologist and a puppy have in common?
A. A wet nose.

Q. What's the best thing about fingering a gypsy during her period?
A. You get your palm red for free.

Q. How do you make a hormone?
A. Don't pay her.

Q. Why is being in the army like a blow-job?
A. The closer you get to discharge, the better you feel.

Q. What's worse than getting raped by Jack the Ripper?
A. Getting fingered by Captain Hook.

Q. Why do Scotsmen wear kilts?
A. Because the sheep can hear a zip a mile away.

Q. What has two grey legs and two brown legs?
A. An elephant with diarrhoea.

Q. What do you call two lesbians on their period?
A. Finger painting.

Q. Why did the lumber truck stop?
A. To let the lumber jack off.

What's the difference between a pop Svengali and a gynaecologist?
A pop Svengali fucks his singers and a gynaecologist sucks his fingers.

First-year students at medical school are receiving their first anatomy class with a dead human body.

They gather around the surgery table with the body covered by a white sheet.

The professor says, "In medicine, you need two qualities. The first is that you must not be disgusted by anything involving the human body."

As an example, the professor pulls back the sheet, sticks his finger in the arse of the corpse, withdraws it and sticks his finger in his mouth.

"Go ahead and do the same thing," he says.

The students hesitate, but eventually take turns sticking a

finger in the arse of the dead body and then sucking on it.

When everyone has finished, the Professor says, "The second most important quality is observation. I stuck in my middle finger and sucked on my index finger. Now learn to pay attention…"

Q. How is a monkey like a chainsaw?
A. They both fuck up trees.

Q. Why do women have two per cent more brains than a cow?
A. So that when you pull their tits they won't shit on the floor.

A man is walking on the beach when he sees a woman with no arms and legs lying by the shore crying.

He says, "What's the matter?"

She says, "I've never been kissed."

So he kneels down and gives her a peck on the lips.

The woman smiles and the man starts to walk away, but after a few steps he hears her crying again.

So he goes back and says, "What's the matter?"

She says, "I've never been screwed."

So the man picks the woman up, throws her in the sea and shouts, "You're screwed now!"

Q. What's the difference between pussy and apple pie?
A. You can eat your mum's apple pie.

Q. What's the only animal with an arsehole in the middle of its back?
A. A police horse.

Three nuns are talking.

The first nun says, "I was cleaning in Father Hilton's room the other day and do you know what I found? A bunch of pornographic magazines."

The second nun says, "What did you do?"

The first nun says, "I threw them in the bin."

The second nun says, "I can top that. I was in Father Hilton's room putting away the laundry and I found a bunch of condoms."

The first nun says, "What did you do?"

The second nun says, "I poked holes in all of them."

The third nun faints.

A man is lying in hospital with an oxygen mask over his mouth and nose, and is still heavily sedated from a four-hour operation.

A young nurse appears to sponge his hands and feet.

"Nurse," the man mumbles from behind the mask, 'are my testicles black?"

Embarrassed, the young nurse says, "I don't know; I'm only here to wash your hands and feet."

He struggles again to ask, "Nurse, are my testicles black?"

So she pulls back the sheets, raises his gown, holds his penis in one hand and his testicles in her other hand, takes a close look and says, "There's nothing wrong with them!"

The man pulls off his oxygen mask and says very slowly, "That felt great – but are… my… test… results… back?"

Have you heard about the new line of tampons that have bells and tinsel?

It's for the Christmas period.

A woman is seriously ill, so her husband takes her to the doctor.

The doctor says, "It's either Alzheimer's or AIDS."

The husband says, "How do we find out which?"

The doctor says, "Go for a long drive in the countryside, have a picnic, then leave her in the field. If she gets home, don't fuck her."

Two paedophiles are sitting on a park bench when an 11-year-old girl walks past.

One says to the other, "She used to be a right goer in her day."

Q. What's the difference between purple and pink?
A. The grip.

Q. What do you get when you cross a rooster with a flea?
A. An itchy cock.

Q. What do you call two skunks in the 69 position?
A. Odour eaters.

After a night out, a man brings his mates back to show off his new house.

The visitors are perplexed by a large gong in the lounge.

One says, "What's that big brass gong for?"

The host says, "That's my Talking Clock."

The guest says, "How does it work?"

The host says, "I'll show you" and gives the gong an ear-shattering blow with an unpadded hammer.

A woman's voice from upstairs screams, "For fuck's sake, it's twenty to two in the fucking morning!"

Q. Why did the snooker player go to the toilet?
A. To pot the brown.

Q. What's soft and warm when you go to bed, but hard and stiff when you wake up?
A. Vomit.

Q. What always starts with a p?
A. A shit.

An arrogant man walks into a wine bar and takes a seat next to an attractive woman.

He gives her a quick glance, then casually looks at his watch.

The woman notices this and says, "Is your girlfriend running late?"

He says, "No, I just brought this state-of-the-art watch and I was testing it."

Intrigued, the woman says, "A state-of-the-art watch? What's so special about it?"

He says, "It uses alpha waves to talk to me telepathically."

She says, "What's it telling you now?"

He says, "It says you're not wearing any knickers."

The woman says, "Well, it must be broken, because actually I am wearing knickers."

The man says, "Bloody thing; must be an hour fast."

Q. What's the best way to cancel an appointment at the sperm bank?
A. Phone up and say you can't come.

Q. What does the receptionist at the sperm clinic say to clients as they're leaving?
A. "Thanks for coming."

Q. What's the worst thing about being a test tube baby?
A. You know for sure that your dad's a wanker.

A woman's having a shower when she slips over on the bathroom floor.

But instead of falling forwards or backwards, she slips sideways, does the splits and suctions herself to the floor.

She yells and her husband comes running.

She says, "I've suctioned myself to the floor!"

He tries to pull her up, but can't.

He says, "You're just too heavy. I'll go across the road and get a mate to help."

He comes back with a mate, but, hard as they pull, they still can't get her off the floor.

The mate says, "I've got an idea."

His husband says, "What's that?"

The mate says, "I'll go home and get my hammer and chisel and we'll break the tiles under her."

The husband says, "OK. While you're doing that, I'll stay here and play with her tits."

The mate says, "Play with her tits? Why?"

The husband says, "Well, if I can get her wet enough, we can slide her into the kitchen where the tiles aren't so expensive."

A waiter is walking around his restaurant when he notices three men at the door masturbating.

He says, "What the hell are you doing?"

The first bloke says, "We saw the notice on your wall saying, 'First come, first served'."

Three old ladies are walking down the street when a man in a dirty raincoat appears and flashes them.

Two have a stroke; one can't reach.

A priest has been in the confessional all day without a break.

He's desperate to take a dump, but people keep coming to confess and he hates to leave.

Eventually, he peers out of his cubicle and signals the janitor to come over. He asks the janitor to cover for him, gives him the confessions book, then rushes off in the direction of the toilet.

The janitor is bewildered, but he goes into the confessional and sits down.

A woman on the other side says, "Bless me, Father, for I

have sinned. I cheated on my husband."

The janitor scans through the book until he finds 'Adultery'. He tells the woman to say 50 Hail Marys and wash in holy water.

Next comes a man who says, "Bless me, Father, for I have sinned. I had oral sex with another man."

The janitor hunts through the book, but he can't find a penance for oral sex.

He leans out of the confessional and whispers to an altar boy, "What does the priest give for oral sex?"

The boy says, "Five quid and a chocolate bar."

Q. What's the difference between a rubber tyre and 365 blow-jobs?
A. One is a Goodyear, the other is a great year.

Q. What sexual position produces the ugliest children?
A. Ask your mum.

Q. Why does your washing machine laugh?
A. It's taking the piss out of your pants.

Two condoms walk past a gay bar. One turns to the other and says, "Fancy going in there and getting shit-faced?"

A hard bloke walks into a brothel holding two unopened bottles of beer and growls, "I'm looking for the roughest, toughest prostitute in town."

The pimp says, "No problem. She's upstairs, second room on the right."

The hard bloke stomps up the stairs, kicks the door open and bellows, "I'm looking for the roughest, toughest prostitute in town."

The woman inside the room says, "You found her!"

She strips naked, bends over and grabs her ankles.

The hard man says, "How do you know I want that position first?"

The prostitute says, "I don't. I just thought you might want to open those beers."

A vampire goes into a pub and asks for some boiling water.

The landlord says, "I thought you only drank blood?"

The vampire pulls out a used tampon and says, "I'm making tea."

Q. What did the vet say to the dog who kept licking his balls?

A. "Thanks!"

A tortoise gets raped by two snails. "Describe them," says the policeman.

"I can't," says the tortoise, "it all happened so fast."

Q. What do you call a Welshman with a sheep under each arm?

A. A pimp.

Q. What do you call a Welshman who owns goats as well as sheep?
A. Bisexual.

Three women are in a bar.

The first says, "I've had sex so many times I can fit four fingers up my vagina."

The second says, "Well, I can fit my whole arm up."

The third women says nothing, while slowly sliding down over her bar stool.

ESSENTIAL TRIVIA FOR THE PUB

Animal Magic

The leopard seal, native to the Antarctic, can consume an entire adélle penguin in four minutes, starting by skinning it alive on the water.

The sugar glider – a type of flying squirrel – can glide up to 148.5ft (45 metres).

Zebras are white with black stripes, not vice versa.

A radar has logged a peregrine falcon making a 1,000ft (305 metre) dive travelling at… 114mph. Which is still short of it's top speed: 124mph.

Goat's eyes have rectangular pupils.

Pandas love porn. A baby boom was sparked by Chinese scientists who showed a handful of the lazy, sex-shy bears a DVD of other pandas mating. The result? Almost a 250 per cent increase in births.

Animals That Might Take Over The World

1. Nine-year-old sea lion Jonao can paint letters. In Chinese. He put the brush in his mouth, and daubed "wild boar" at Hakkeijima Sea Paradise in suburban Tokyo. Today "wild boar", tomorrow… "attack the humans"?

2. Since 1935, cane toads introduced to Australia have multiplied at such a rate that now (population 200 million and destroying *everything* in their path), the Australian military has been called in to halt their advance on Darwin.

3. Animals can TALK. In English! A captive African grey parrot discovered in 2004 called N'kisi has an astonishing 950 word vocabulary. He uses words in context, with past, present and future tense, and even has a sense of humour.

4. Other creatures aren't far behind. South America's giant river otters have nine distinct vocalisations, which vary from screams of excitement to coos of recognition.

5. Earthquakes will decimate our cities and us, but not snakes. The spineless serpents can enjoy our planet once we're gone – they detect tremors up to 75 miles away, five days before it kicks off. At which point, they leave their nests en masse.

In 1945 a chicken survived for two years after having its head cut off. The axe missed the jugular vein and left enough of the brain stem for the poultry to survive.

Each year, insects eat one third of the Earth's entire food crop.

Of all known forms of animal ever to inhabit the Earth, only about 10 per cent still exist today.

There are only two known animals with blue tongues: the black bear and the chow dog.

As of December 2006, China has fluorescent pigs. The DNA of a bioluminescent jellyfish was implanted in to a sow and three piglets were born 114 days later with mouths, trotters and hooves that glow green under UV light.

In the last 4,000 years, no new animals have been domesticated.

A walrus tusk can grow up to one metre in length.

A New York man blinded in his right eye 64 years ago by WWII shrapnel regained his sight after being head butted by a pedigree racehorse.

The Yanomami Indians of South America call the jaguar "Eater of Souls", due to their belief that it consumes the spirits of the dead.

Wildlife In Numbers

20lb lost by Pongo the dalmatian to win the accolade of Britain's Top Pet Slimmer 2006.

47 Average number of teeth in a mosquito's mouth.

80 live rats escaped on a Saudi Airlines flight at 25,000ft late last year.

5 million Average number of eggs laid in one go by the mola mola, or ocean sunfish.

7 feet length of the carpet pythons found in an Australian school teacher's U-bend after she complained of a blockage.

60mph Maximum flight speed of the dragonfly.

0.0313mph speed of the fastest-moving the common garden snail – which is the fastest snail.

14 million camels on planet Earth.

250niles miles a king penguin will travel in search of food for its chick.

200,000 Glasses of milk a cow will fill during her lifetime.

26 Cycles per second a cat purrs at, frequency fans. Which is the same cycle rate as an idling diesel engine.

1 millions dogs in the US estimated to be named as the primary beneficiary in their owner's will.

Goats do not eat tin cans. They simply nibble at them for the tasty glue found beneath the labels.

Emus cannot walk backwards.

The honey possum has the largest testes to body size of any mammal. Its balls weigh 4.2 per cent of its body weight.

The northern right whale is named thus only because hunters originally thought it the "right whale" to kill.

Snow leopards can bring down prey up to three times their own size.

All porcupines float in water.

The Arctic fox can withstand temperatures as low as −50 degrees Celsius.

The chiffchaff – a small bird that visits the UK in the summer – is so-called as its two-note song sounds like 'chiff chaff'.

The world's heaviest insect is the wetapunga (also known as the demon grasshopper). The largest ever on record weighed 71g.

The world's smallest primate is the pygmy mouse lemur. They measure just 6.1cm.

Ratty from Wind In The Willows was actually a water vole, not a rat. The creatures are commonly mistaken for one another.

The bones of a pigeon weigh less than its feathers.

Tiger sharks are nicknamed "the dustbin of the sea" as they not only eat anything in their path including other sharks, but also eat rubbish itself.

Neither rats, rabbits nor horses can vomit.

Madagascar's fat-tailed dwarf lemurs hibernate surviving only on the fat in their tails.

Jungle cats – native to Egypt, the Middle East, southern Asia and western China – are the only cats that bark.

The common goldfish is the only animal that can see both infra-red and ultra-violet light.

Unlike domestic turkeys fattened up for festive slaughter, wild turkeys can fly short distances at speeds up to 55mph.

The poisonous copperhead snake smells like freshly cut cucumbers.

A pregnant goldfish is called a twit.

Twelve or more cows are known as a flink.

The poisonous copperhead snake smells like freshly cut cucumbers.

The largest animal ever seen alive was a 113.5 foot, 170-ton female blue whale.

Cats in Halifax, Nova Scotia, have a very high probability of having six toes.

Motor Madness

The McLaren F1's engine bay is lined with 24 carat gold foil.

The Jaguar XJ220 never lived up to its name because it never did 220 mph. F1 racer Martin Brundle manager to coax 217.1 mph out of it.

The original Golf GTI weighed a mere 810 kg. The current Mk V model GTI is 526 kg heavier.

Fernando Alonso drove the same Renault F1 car in every Grand Prix in 2006.

The paddle-shift transmission in a Ferrari 599 GTB can change gears in 100 milliseconds, almost as fast as an F1 car.

The first Porsche 911 Turbo launched in 1974 has 256 bhp and topped out at 155 mph. The current Turbo has 480 mph and a 195 mph top speed.

At 3.2 seconds the Caterham R500 is quicker to 60 mph than a McLaren F1 and Ferrari Enzo.

A top-fuel dragster will hit 170 mph in 7.9 seconds.

The Volkswagen Beetle was in continuous production for 58 years – the longest run of any car ever.

The Lexus Ls is fitted with a 19 speaker Mark Levinson stereo hooked up to a hard drive capable of holding up to 4000 songs.

The Fiat 500 of 1957 was powered by an air-cooled two-cylinder engine that produced just 13bhp for a 55mph top speed.

In 1987 a Bugatti Royale Kelner Coupe sold at auction for £4,913,000, the most expensive car to ever go under the hammer.

Between 1908 and 1927, 15million Model T Fords were produced.

Xenon headlamp bulbs are about the size of a match head and need around 25,000volts to produce any light.

Stuffed with expensive impact monitoring equipment, the average crash test dummy costs £100,000.

The Knowledge test every London black cab driver must pass involves knowing every street within a six-mile radius of Charing Cross.

Audi's Quattro all-wheel-drive system was designed by VW boss Ferdinand Piech, the same man who instigated the Bugatti Veyron and purchased Bentley, Lamborghini and Cosworth.

In Japan, Toyota sells cars called the Windom, Belta, Kluger, Funcargo and Ractis.

The Bugatti Type 35 of 1924 was the most successful racing car of all time, racking up 1000 wins in five years.

On full afterburn, the Thrust SSC's twin Spey 205 jet engines each produce 25,000 lb of thrust, around 55,000 bhp.

The 1965 Renault 16 was the world's first five-door hatchback.

British sports car marque TVR was named after its founder TreVoR Wilkinson.

Honda has never had a single warranty claim on any of its V-TEC engines.

When Vauxhall launched the 176-mph Lotus Carlton, The *Daily Mail* was so incensed by its top speed that it mounted a public campaign to have it banned.

The Ferrari FXX has 40% more downforce than a standard Enzo.

The 350-mph JCB Dieselmax world speed record holder is powered by two engines, each producing 750 bhp.

The Quandt family, which owns just under half of BMW, is valued at £10 billion.

The Heuer Monaco, the watch immortalised by Steve McQueen in *Le Mans,* was the first automatic chronograph in the world.

Honda turned to F1 world champion Ayrton Senna to help design its NSX supercar.

The Porsche GT3 RS has a plastic rear windscreen to save weight.

In 1996, 1997 and 1998 Maserati did not sell a single car in the UK.

The Bugatti Veyron

1. With a 0-62mph time of 2.5seconds, the Veyron is quicker off the mark than a F18 Hornet jet fighter accelerating for take-off on full afterburners.
2. The Bugatti's W16 engine is actually two twin-turbo 4.0-litre V8 engines mounted alongside each other on a common crankcase.
3. To achieve full speed, the driver has to switch on a Speed Key, which retracts the rear spoiler to reduce drag and boost speed.
4. The mid-mounted engine has no cover – the polished aluminium alloy air intakes and cam covers are open to the elements to help keep the engine cool.
5. At full throttle in seventh gear the Veyron returns 2.8mpg, which means it run its 22-gallon fuel tank dry in just 20minutes.

Audi's mid-engined R8 supercar features an incredible 210 external LED lights used in the head and tail lamps and *to illuminate the engine bay so other drivers can see the engine at night.*

After the film *Goldfinger* was launched, in which James Bond drove an Aston Martin DB5, Aston's sales rocketed by 60%.

Motoring In Numbers

13,5million – the number of driver who had points put on their licence in 2006.

86,400 – the cost in pounds of the M6 Convertible, BMW's most expensive car.

1369 – the number of F1 points Michael Schumacher scored in his career, the highest to date.

137 – the number of times a second each rotor in the Mazda RX-8's engine turns at peak power.

140 – the number of horsepower VW managers to squeeze out of its tiny 1.4-litre supercharged and turbocharged Golf engine.

6.75 – the size in litres of the Rolls-Royce Phantom Drophead's V12 engine.

60 – the number of seconds it takes Toyota's Valenciennes factory in France to produce one Yaris.

8 – the number of forward gears in the Lexus LS460's gearbox.

16 – the number of model types in the Mercedes range, more than any other carmaker in the UK.

18.9 – the average number of miles the Range Rover Vogue can travel on one gallon of petrol.

20 – the percentage of people killed in car crashes with illegal drugs in their blood stream.

1012 – the number of horsepower the Bristol Fighter S's biturbo 8.0-litre V10 produces.

350.8 – the speed in miles per hour that Chris Carr achieved on his Streamliner motorbike to set a new land speed motorbike record late last year.

170 – the speed in miles per hour of the Lamborghini Miura, the world's first supercar.

The Ferrari F40 was the first supercar to break the 200mph barrier with a 201 mph top speed, 3mph more than its deadliest rival the Porsche 959.

The first supercar was the 350 bhp V12 Lamborghini Muira, which made its debut in 1966. *CAR* magazine coined the term 'supercar' to describe it.

During a pedestrian impact, small explosive charges in the Jaguar XK's bonnet fire to pop up the bonnet and protect the pedestrian's head from the engine.

The Bugatti EB110's tiny 2.5-litre V12 engine used four turbochargers to produce a massive 553 bhp.

Knight Rider's KITT car took its name from the acronym of Knight Industries Two Thousand.

BP's *Ultimate 102* petrol costs two and a half times the cost of regular unleaded.

Pub Games

1. Bullshit Poker

Each player has a note in his hand (originally a dollar bill) and takes in turns to make bids of the highest "hand" in the combined notes – one might bid four 7s, the next three 8s, another four 8s, and the last guy a pair of 10s (represented by 0s, 1s, aces, are high). Eventually someone challenges this with a "Bullshit!". If it's actually true, you each pay the bidder, if it's not, he pays each of you.

2. Spoof

You all have three coins in one hand. Transfer between none and three to your right hand and hold it out, closed. Take it in turns to guess how many total coins there are in all fists. Get it right and you drop out. Last man in buys the next round.

3. Big Lebowski

You have to match the Dude drink for drink (White Russians – vodka, Kahlua, milk). Some naughty folk also match him toke for toke.

4. Yard of Ale

Try to beat the last world records listed (5.5 seconds for a three-pint yard set by a drinker at Corby Town FC, 5 seconds for the 2.5pint by RAF Upper Heyford, both from 1976) before Guinness succumbed to "responsible drinking" pressure in the 90s.

5. The Beer Hunter

Russian roulette with a four-pack instead of a pistol. One can gets shaken up, then everyone takes a can at random and opens it while pointing at your head.

6. Drink While You Think

The first player names a celebrity, say Ricky Gervais, then the next has to name one whose first name starts with the same letter as the surname, so George Michael. If the next player uses a one-named celeb, say Madonna, it carries on with M as the first initial; if it's a double letter, say Mandy Moore, it bounces it back the way it came. You drink while it's your turn till you say a name. In the extreme version, other players can be shouting names you can't have.

7. Roxanne

Divide your group into two teams and put Roxanne by The Police on the jukebox/stereo. When Sting sings "Roxanne", one team drinks; when the he sings "Put on the red light", the other team drinks. Simple.

8. Star Wars

Drink every time the Force is mentioned. In the original films, drink every time some one says "Luke". In Episodes I-III, swap that for Anekin.

9. Headmaster

As an addition to any other drinking game, one player is the "headmaster". When he puts his head on the table, the last person to get their head down has to skull. Usually ends up with a couple headbutting the table.

Space: the Final Frontier

The Moon was created when the early Earth banged into another early version of a planet. A chunk of planet was spat out and got caught in the Earth's gravitational pull.

So far, 209 planets outside our galaxy have been discovered. Most are bigger than Jupiter, the biggest planet in our Solar System.

The craters on the moon are a result of asteroids and comets smashing into it over the last few billion years. The lack of any atmosphere or weather means they've all been preserved. The largest crater is 13km deep and 2,240km across – about 50 times the size of the UK.

The Outer Space Treaty – signed by all major countries in 1967 – means no-one is allowed to claim any part of the moon's surface. It also means weapons or any form of military installation are forbidden.

The Moon is 384,399 km away from Earth, meaning it takes light reflected off the Moon's surface 1.3 seconds to reach us.

Despite only being roughly eleven times bigger in size, Jupiter weighs 317 times as much as Earth.

Pluto was considered the most distant of the nine planets in the Solar System until last year, when an official definition of a planet was drawn up by the International Astronomical Union. It's now considered to be a "dwarf planet".

Earth only has one moon. Jupiter has 63 and Saturn has 56.

Man has not visited any other planet yet – only the Moon.

The further away a planet is from the Sun, the longer its year. A year on Neptune, 30 times further from the Sun than us, the most distant planet, is the equivalent to 164 years on Earth. A day on Venus is the equivalent to 243 days.

The Sun accounts for 99.86% of the Solar System's total mass. Jupiter and Saturn account for more than 90% of the remaining mass.

The Sun is roughly halfway through its life. It was only 75 per cent as bright early in its history and it's getting brighter as it gets older. In about five billion years, it will blow up

Venus is the planet closest to Earth, but being a bit closer to the Sun, it gets hotter: about 400 degrees C.

The temperature on the surface of the Sun is thought to be about 5,727 degrees C.

The Solar System – In proportion

the Sun = Big Ben's clock face
Jupiter = Standard car wheel
Saturn = Large Domino's Pizza
Uranus = Basketball
Neptune = Football
Earth = Tennis ball
Venus = Orange
Mars = Golf ball
Mercury = Polo mint
The Moon = 5p piece

TV & Comedy

Jack Dee has appeared on Jonathan Ross's chat show six times – the most sofa spots by any celebrity.

Every episode of *Seinfeld* contains a small homage to Superman – whether it's a mention of him, a background picture or even Jerry wearing red and blue.

Little Britain sketches filmed on the same day in the same swimming pool filled two of the top five places in Channel 4's *50 Greatest Comedy Sketches Of All Time* poll – Lou and Andy's diving board gag and Vicky Pollard pissing in the water.

Matt Lucas's cousin, Alexa Tilley, was a contestant on *The Apprentice*. Alan Sugar told her, "You're fired".

The live stage show of *Bottom* was so violent that both Ade Edmonson and Rik Mayall were hospitalised at various times.

The *Father Ted* theme tune was written and performed by The Divine Comedy and a version of it appears on their *Casanova* album, along with a track called 'Woman Of The World', their first stab at the theme tune – which had already been rejected.

The poster behind Larry's secretary's desk in *Curb Your Enthusiasm* changes every episode.

Jennifer Saunders got her *Absolutely Fabulous* character's name, Edina Monsoon, from her husband Ade Edmonson's university nickname, Eddie Monsoon.

Dave Gorman prepares for live shows in his dressing room by balancing pebbles on top of each other.

Jerry Springer – The Opera creator Stewart Lee compulsively collects all the miniature toiletries in every hotel he stays in.

Ricky Gervais's 80s New Romantic band Seona Dancing only had one top 10 hit – in the Philippines.

Jimmy Carr has a pink orchid named after him.

Thick Of It and *Day Today* creator Armando Iannucci was offered the Radio 1 breakfast show in the 1990s – after he had refused it went to Steve Wright instead.

Two thieves were jailed after stealing £200,000 from Ricky Gervais's bank account, using a picture from one of his DVDs pasted into a dead man's passport as ID.

In 2005 Sacha Baron Cohen returned to the Israeli kibbutz where he spent part of his gap year and coached the Frisbee team to a tournament victory.

Ant and Dec have taken out insurance so each gets a £2 million payout if the other one dies unexpectedly.

Before he was famous, Jerry Seinfeld made money selling fake jewellery and was involved in a telemarketing scam.

Father Ted co-creator Graham Linehan based the Father Jack Hackett character on one of the priests at his secondary school.

There are two statues of comedians in Douglas on the Isle Of White – one of Norman Wisdom, one of George Formby. There are none in Norwich, after the City Council refused to give planning permission for a 60-foot statue of Alan Partridge.

Mirth In Numbers

2 – fans who turned up to a Ben Elton book signing in Carlisle in January 2006.

16 – times black comedian Damon Wayons dropped the "n-bomb" at LA's *Laugh Factory* the week after Michael 'Kramer' Richards' racist rant. It earned Wayans a fine and a suspension from the venue, whose owners had banned the word, but he said, "I'll be damned if the white man uses that word last."

95% – University Of Maryland test subjects whose blood flow was increased by watching comedy, equivalent to mild aerobic exercise.

201 – Swear words used in a single TV show (one every nine seconds), a world record set by Paul Kay in *Strutter*, beating *South Park*'s previous best, 162.

In a deleted scene on the *Pirates of the Caribbean* DVD, *Fast Show* obsessive Johnn Depp uses the "I'll get me coat" catchphrase.

Prince Philip protested that Catherine Tate had gone too far during the Royal Variety Show when her "bovvered" character Lauren commented that "the old fella next to the Queen" appeared to be asleep.

Peep Show's Mitchell and Webb wrote sketches for *Armstrong & Miller*, *Dead Ringers* and *Big Train*.

Pop piss-taker Weird Al Jankovic failed to get clearance to release a James Blunt parody single called 'You're Pitiful'.

Stephen Fry was not originally intended to be the host of the show *QI* – the producers had wanted Michael Palin.

Zeppo Marx invented the bomb clasps ('Marman clamps') on the bomber *Enola Gay*, which released the A-bomb over Hiroshima.

The only one *Blackadder* series where Edmund Blackadder does not die at the end is the third, when he plays the Prince Regent's butler.

Jimmy Carr got 4 A grades at A-level.

When *Fawlty Towers* is broadcast in Spain, waiter Manuel's nationalty is changed to Italian.

Men Behaving Badly star Martin Clunes collects and restores VW camper vans.

Writer John Sullivan initially gave *Only Fools and Horses* the working title *Readies* but eventually decided a longer name would grab viewers' attention.

The Vicar Of Dibley is filmed in Turville in Buckinghamshire – also the location of *Midsomer Murders*.

Fast Show star Simon Day claimed based his 'Competitive Dad' character on a man he once saw at a swimming pool, who challenged his two young children to a race and then swam away at top speed, leaving them struggling at the other end.

The shop used in the exterioor shots in *Open All Hours* is actually a hairdressers.

The four most common references in Eddie Izzard's stand-up routines, according to avid fans, are jam, banjos, bananas and the Bible.

Chris Morris's strict Jesuit religious school, Stoneyhurst, was the subject of a police investigation into child abuse – pupils were allegedly beaten with a whale bone.

A script assistant tried to sue the producers of *Friends* for sexual harrassment because of the rude jokes she had to type out during script meetings – she lost.

In 1997 *The Chris Rock Show* ran a joke about an OJ Simpson instructional video called "I didn't murder my wife but if I had, this is how I'd have done it" – nine years before OJ wrote a book about exactly that.

Comedy In Numbers

2 – heart attacks suffered by Richard Pryor, in a life also featuring six divorces, eight children, a prostitute mother and near-fatal burns from freebasing.

7.5 – Years longer than the actual Korean War (three years) that *M*A*S*H* ran on TV.

38 million – dollars made by the Original Kings Of Comedy tour, featuring *Ocean's Eleven* star Bernie Mac and three other leading black comedians. It became the most successful comedy tour ever.

150 – one-liners (sample: "I put instant coffee in a microwave – I nearly went back in time") told by stone-faced Steven Wright in his 60-minute US TV special.

230 – F-words used by Eddie Murphy in the stage show *Delirious*.

300 million – pounds raised by *Comic Relief* since it started in 1985.

700 – lengths of an Olympic swimming pool equivalent to the 22-mile cross-Channel swim completed by David Walliams

5 – foreign versions of *The Office*: the US version with Steve Carell, the French *Le Bureau* (Brent is called David Gervais), French-Canadian *La Job*, plus German and Brazilian comedies strongly modelled on it.

7 – British Comedy Awards won by David Walliams and Matt Lucas, more than anyone else. Ant & Dec are second with 6.

Peter Kay is a qualified stand-up comedian... it was a module on his Media Performance Studies BTec course.

MPs recently voted *Yes Minister* the best political comedy, ahead of *Spitting Image* and *Bremner, Bird and Fortune*, but *The Thick Of It* didn't make the top 10.

Peep Show creator Sam Bain's granny was one of the old ladies who were permanent residents at *Fawlty Towers*.

Russell Brand is a vicar – at least he has been ordained as a minister over the internet so he could officiate at a friend's wedding.

Torchwood's Captain Jack, John Barrowman, was down to the last three to play Will in *Will & Grace* but was rejected for not being gay enough. The part went to the straight Eric McCormack.

Ardal O'Hanlon's dad is the Speaker of the Daíl, the Irish House Of Commons.

Michael Palin once appeared in a cameo as a nervous British surfer in *Home And Away*.

The face of Dale Gribble, the conspiracy theorist neighbour in *King Of The Hill*, is based on *T-1000* actor Robert Patrick.

Dylan Moran, stand-up and red wine-swilling Bernard from *Black Books*, got married on the day of Princess Diana's funeral, not far from Westminster Abbey.

In a *Spaced* spoof of a scene from *The Sixth Sense*, the dead cyclist who appears at Simon Pegg's window is played by Olivia Williams – who plays Bruce Willis' wife in the original film.

The *Futurama* theme tune samples the drums from James Brown's *Funky Drummer*.

Royston Vasey, the village in *The League Of Gentlemen*, is the real name of comedian Roy 'Chubby' Brown, who plays its mayor.

The music in *South Park* whenever Satan's son Damien appears sounds like the scary 'Ave Satani' from *The Omen* but in fact they are chanting "Rectus Dominus [ass master]… Cheesy Poofs".

Bill Gates' personal fortune is five times the Gross Domestic Product of Iceland. He's given away over $29 billion to charities since 2000.

An average of $2 million per 30 seconds was paid for advertisers for slots during the last-ever episode of *Friends*. The show was seen by 51.1 million Americans..

Five Nuggets about *The Simpsons*

1. Names of characters have been known to change – Mafia boss Fat Tony's surname has been Balducci, D'Amico and Williams. Krusty's real name has been both Herschel Schmoikel Krustofski and Herschel Pinkus Yerucham Krustofski.
2. Only Homer, Bart and Lisa have dialogue in every episode (Marge appears but does not speak in "Krusty Gets Kancelled").
3. Creator Matt Groening named "Bart The Daredevil" (where Bart attempts to jump Springfield Gorge on his skateboard) as his "best episode ever".
4. The family's middle names are JoJo (Bart), Marie (Lisa) and simply J (Homer). Marge and Maggie have none.
5. The characters were originally drawn with yellow skin to attract the attention of channel-hoppers.

Movie Trivia

Brad Pitt is a trained journalist who dropped out towards the end of his Missouri University degree to pursue acting.

Simon Pegg is the godfather of Chris Martin and Gwyneth Paltrow's daughter Apple.

In the Bond film *View To A Kill*, one of Christopher Walken's KGB bodyguards is Dolph Lundgren.

1995 Geena Davis-vehicle *Cutthroat Island* cost $100 million to produce and promote but earned back only $11 million – making it the biggest-ever box-office loser.

007 Daniel Craig's middle name is Wroughton.

Jack Black's parents were both rocket scientists.

Hugh Jackman wasn't supposed to be Wolverine in the X-Men films. He was a last-minute addition when Brit actor Dougray Scott dropped out.

Clint Eastwood once beat up four sailors in a bar for "having bad manners".

Tom Cruise makes a cameo in *Young Guns*, but you have to look closely. After dropping by on set, the director agreed he could make appear but only if he wore a really big moustache.

Matt Damon was originally down to play Daredevil but the role eventually went to his real-life best friend Ben Affleck.

In *Back To The Future*, when Michael J. Fox visits Doc Brown's house, one of the clocks hanging of the wall has a clock featuring a little man hanging off one of the hands. This directly references the end of the film.

In *The Big Lebowski*, you don't see The Dude bowl at any point during the film.

Sylvester Stallone and Arnold Schwarzenegger were supposed to be the actors who had their faces switched in the eventual Nicholas Cage/John Travolta film *Face/Off*.

In *Die Hard*, the Nakatomi building where Bruce Willis kicks arse in actually 20th Century Fox's head office.

One of the ninja-style guards Bruce Lee fights – and then puts in a headlock – in *Enter The Dragon* is none other than Jackie Chan.

Harrison Ford's second wife Melissa Mathison wrote the screenplay for *ET*.

***Ghostbusters'* food-scoffing phantom Slimer was actually called Onionhead. It wasn't until the cartoon came out that his name was changed to Slimer**

The school in *Ferris Bueller's Day Off* is the same one used in The Breakfast Club.

Ed Norton's character in *Fight Club* doesn't have a name.

The lumberjack who gets his arm ripped out of its socket arm-wrestling Jeff Goldblum in *The Fly* is George Chuvalo, who fought Muhammad Ali for the world heavyweight title in 1966.

In *The Godfather*, the horse head that film boss Jack Waltz finds in his bed was real. The crew found the horse in a New Jersey rendering plant and had its head packed in ice and shipped to the set.

In *Halloween*, serial killer Michael Myers wears a mask of Captain Kirk that's been painted white.

In *Kill Bill: Volume I*, Uma Thurman drives past a wall featuring a "Red Apples" cigarette ad. "Red Apples" are a fictional brand that Quentin Tarantino uses in all his films.

In *Lord of the Rings: The Fellowship of the Ring*, you can see a car in the distant background as Frodo leaves his home in the shire.

At the end of *Rocky V*, The Italian Stallion was supposed to die in Adrian's arms after being beaten to death by "Tommy Gunn" but the producers thought it was too downbeat.

In the opening minutes of *Saving Private Ryan*, the soldiers who have their limbs blown off are real amputees. Spielberg did this to make his film more realistic

Film In Numbers

$100 million – Bruce Willis's fee for *The Sixth Sense*, the highest salary for an actor of all-time.

91 – times police were called on Sacha Baron Cohen during the filming of *Borat*.

10 – Leonardo DiCaprio's age when his agent suggested he change his name to the more American-friendly Lenny Williams. DiCaprio declined.

$20million – amount in dollars Robert De Niro was paid to appear in the 2005 Ben Stiller comedy *Meet The Fockers*.

6 – words used by producers to pitch *Talladega Nights* to the studio: "Will Ferrell as a Nascar driver".

4 – months added to the making of Mel Gibson's *Apocalypto* after torrential rains in Mexico halted production.

9 – cast and crew members who died during the making of *The Exorcist*.

16 – lines Arnie has in the first *Terminator* film

237 – number of both Red's prison cell in *The Shawshank Redemption* and the hotel room Jack Nicholson is forbidden to enter in *The Shining*. Stephen King wrote the stories on which both films were based.

In *The Passion of The Christ*, the hand that nails Jesus to the cross is Mel Gibson's.

Money Matters

During the Civil War period, the Bureau of Engraving and Printing was called upon to print paper notes in denominations of 3 cents, 5 cents, 10 cents, 25 cents, and 50 cents. People hoarded coins because of their intrinsic value which created a drastic shortage of circulating coins.

MTV was offered to CNN media mogul Ted Turner before it launched in 1981 for half a million dollars. Turner refused thinking it was "A complete joke and a failure waiting to happen".

It costs 5.7 cents per note to produce American paper currency.

The world's highest denomination note is the Hungarian 100 million B-Pengo, issued in 1946. That's 100,000,000,000,000,000,000 pengo.
On 2 May 2 1990, John Goddard was mugged at knife-point during his daily courier round from Sheppard's money brokers in London. His briefcase contained bearer bonds worth a total of £292 million.

Gary Glitter's autobiography reveals him so caught up in image that he felt it was his 'duty to his fans' to drink vintage champagne at over £2,000 a bottle at all times.

The most expensive hotel in the world is the Emirates Palace in Abu Dhabi. It costs over £8,000 a night to stay there.

The world's most expensive phone number was auctioned for charity in Qatar last year. The number, 666 6666, sold for £1.5m.

The most expensive residence in the world is Updown Court in Windlesham, Surrey. Currently valued at £70 million, it has 103 rooms including squash court, bowling alley, heated marble driveway, five swimming pools, 24-carat gold leafing on the study's mosaic floor and an underground garage with room for eight limousines.

The Japanese Government issued bank notes, known as Japanese Invasion Money (JIMs) during WWII in its five occupied territories.

In response to the 2004 Asian tsunami, governments worldwide pledged enormous sums of aid but most ended up paying much less. Germany came out worst, paying only 26.2% of the $313 million they promised.

Rolling Stones guoitarist Keith Richards' weekly bills between in 1971 were: £1,000 on food, £1,000 alcohol, £2,500 drugs and £2,500 rent on his a Cote d'Azur villa. Fortunately this total was less than a third of his weekly income.

U2 were the world's top-earning music act in 2005 with an income of £146,371,252.

On average across Europe, men still earn 15% more than woman. The disparity is worst in Germany, where there is a 23% gap.

There were more £20 notes issued in 2006 (341 million) than any other note.

With a wealth of £14.9 billion, steel magnate Lakshmi Mittal is the richest man in Britain, followed by Roman Abramovich with £10.8 billion.

The poorer half of the world's population own barely 1% of global wealth.

Luxembourg has the highest minimum monthly wage in the world of £1,002. Romania's is £49.

The world's wealthiest university, Harvard University in Massachusetts, has a bigger budget than 142 countries, including Cuba, Jordan and Lithuania.

Economists predicted that the World Cup in 2006 generated 900 million pounds for the Brirish economy solely through sales of barbeque food, snacks and beer.

Five Nuggets About The Cost Of The War In Iraq

1. Joseph Stiglitz, former chief economist of the World Bank and winner of the Nobel Prize for Economics, says the total costs of the Iraq War on the US economy will be between $1 trillion and $2 trillion.
2. As of March 2006, £4.5 billion had been spent by the UK in Iraq, all from a government fund called the "Special Reserve" which has a current allocation of £6.44 billion.
3. About $2 billion worth of military equipment is wearing out or being destroyed every month in Iraq and Afghanistan. American charities such as Bake Sales For Body Armour, Soldiers' Angels and Aoperation Helment (a favourite of Cher) have sprung up to provide replacement gear.
4. The current US budget for the Iraq War includes $2.5 billion to combat roadside bombs and other improvised explosive devices, and $2.7 billion for intelligence activities.
5. The war costs American taxpayers $195,000 per day. One day in Iraq could feed all of the starving children in the world today almost four and a half times over.

The difference in prize money between finishing 4th and 5th in the Premiership is a staggering £26.5 million pounds. The difference between finishing 5th and 6th is just £2.6 million.

In March 2006, Amanda Newkirk, a 7-month pregnant, 19 year-old waitress in Virginia, was left $1,000 to cover a $26.35 with a note saying "Keep the change! Have a great day".

It costs £39 to be a member of the Labour party, but only £15 to become a signed-up Conservative and £6 to join the Liberal Democrats.

Grey Goose vodka creator Sidney Frank bought a $400,000 black 2004 Mercedes Maybach and paid an extra $100,000 to make it bulletproof. The cushy ride features reclinable airline-style seats. The booze billionaire flies the car back and forth between his New York and San Diego homes. He also uses it to travel to golf courses, where he pays a team of professional golfers to play for his amusement.

The term 'buck' originated from the Old West when buckskin was a common medium of barter exchange with Indians.

The most expensive city in Britain to buy heroin and coaine is Belfast (£100 and £55 per gram respectively).

Last year 454,000 Britons did all their Christmas shopping on Christmas Eve.

Salt was used as a currency in pre-coinage Europe.

People & Places

Now-divorced Kid Rock and Pamela Anderson read their wedding vows to each other off their Blackberries.

Brazil is named after the nut, not the other way round.

Nobody know for sure why penguins are called penguins. It might be from the Latin 'pinguis', meaning fat, or from the Welsh 'pen gwyn', meaning white head.

The average person only feels 'adult' when they hit the age of 24, according to psychological studies.

Merry Clayton, who sang backing vocals on "Gimme Shelter" by The Rolling Stones, suffered a miscarriage due to the intensity of her performance.

Every US president with a beard has been a Republican.

According to English law, all males under 14 have to do two hours of longbow practise per week supervised by a local clergyman.

Humans have four nostrils. We have two internal nostrils called choannae.

James is the most common name for a criminal.

Time Magazine's 'Man of the Year' in 1938 was Adolf Hitler.

Men spend approximately two years of their life in the toilet.

The highest mountain in the solar system is on Mars. Mount Olympus is 14 miles high and 388 miles across, almost three times the size of Mount Everest.

The Eiffel Tower grows seven inches in the summer.

Dave, of legendary Cockney-knees-up duo Chas and Dave, is not a Cockney.

The only band member without a beard in ZZ TOP is called Frank Beard.

The dot over the letter 'i' is called a tittle.

The Swiss are the only European nation who eat dogs.

Elvis Presley's manager, Colonel Tom Parker, covered all bases by selling 'I Hate Elvis' badges as well as 'I Love Elvis' ones.

The moon smells like gunpowder.

Entourage star Jeremy Piven's Range Rover has the personalised number plate PIVWEELZ.

People with an IQ of 140-plus are more likely to be left-handed than right-handed, despite lefties only making up 12% of the population.

2006 was the hottest year since records began in 1659.

Around Britain

Hull is the most stupid place in Britain, according to a combination of exam results, numbers of locals with degrees and performance in BBC IQ quiz *Test the Nation*.

Women in Bangor have been voted the ugliest in Britain. The North Wales city beat Gloucester, Exeter, Belfast, Plymouth, Glasgow and Hull to the title.

By law, all black London taxis must carry a bale of hay and a sack of oats.

Norwich is the most badly behaved city in Britain, according to the ratio of population to minor misdemeanour.

TV chef Jean-Christophe Novelli liked his meal at Hemel Hampstead's Restaurant *65* so much that he left a £900 tip.

London has Euro's highest human-to-rat ratio, with 9 million rats to only 7 million humans. You're never more than 10 metres from a rat in the capital.

Amy Winehouse went to Croydon's Brits school – which has also given us Katie Melua, the Kooks and the Feeling.

Of all the world's cities, the word 'porn' is most frequently searched for in Birmingham. Manchester is 2nd and Brentford 8th.

There is only one registered sperm donor in Oxfordshire, making it the UK region that's officially meanest with jizz.

There is a Yorkshire rose in the middle of the 20p coin.

Sunderland is the most sexually frustrated city in Britian, with eight out of ten people saying they're dissatisfied with the sex they're getting.

Bradford is the sexiest city in the UK, with 23% of residents claiming they shag daily.

There were 132 'big cat' sightings in Devon in 2006 – the most in the United Kingdom.

There are more speed cameras in Mid- and South Wales (377) than any other region in the UK. The lowest is Hertfordshire with only 31.

There are more pubs and bars per square mile in Nottingham than in any other European city.

Edinburgh was the first city in the world to have its own fire-brigade.

World Of Sport

Until 1967, it wasn't illegal for Olympic athletes to use drugs to enhance their performance during competition.

Mary Queen of Scots, the first known female golfer, coined the term "caddy" in 1552, calling her assistants cadets. During her reign, the famous golf course at St. Andrews was built.

Tim Henman's great grandmother Ellen Mary Stawell-Brown was, in 1901, the first woman to use an overarm serve at Wimbledon.

West Bromwich Albion play at the highest altitude in the English League, at 551 ft above sea level.

Andrew Strauss has won 75 per cent of Test matches he has captained – the most by any skipper under coach Duncan Fletcher.

Two Juventus youth team players died after trying to retrieve a ball from a lake at the club's Turin training ground.

Extreme Body Parts

Neck
England prop Andrew Sheridan had some fairly impressive stats – the 215 kg he benchpresses means he could qualify for GB's Olympic weight-lifting team – but it's all based on the power that comes from the 8.5-inch-thick wedge of muscle he disguised as a neck. The average male collar size is 16 inches; Sheridan had shirts made with a 21-inch collar.

Heart
Miguel Indurain won five consecutive Tour de Frances in the 1990s – partly because his heart was 50 per cent bigger than most people's. His resting heart rate of 28-29 beats per minute meant he was almost clinically dead. A normal rate is about 70 bpm.

Elbow
The combination of a naturally crooked elbow (it's 32 degrees away from the norm) and a double-jointed wrist means Sri Lankan wizard Muttiah Muralitharan can spin the ball unlike anyone else (Warne included). It's brought him 674 Test wickets and so much controversy that he was forced to bowl in a metal brace in 2004 to prove he doesn't chuck the ball.

Hand
His height (7ft 2ins) and weight (24st) probably help, but it's with his massive fists that Nikolai Valuev has battered his way to the world heavyweight title. Held next to each other,

his clenched fists measure a whole foot across, making them literally twice as big as yours.

Thighs
The reason Real Madrid and Brazil full-back Roberto Carlos (occasionally) hits free-kicks at face-threatening speed? His absurdly large thighs. They're 24 inches in diameter, the same size as Muhammad Ali's when he was heavyweight champ. Pretty impressive when you consider that Ali was nine inches and five stone bigger than Carlos.

Feet
With 22 world records, Aussie swimmer Ian 'Thorpedo' Thorpe is the closest thing to a fish that the human race has ever produced. The biggest similarity to sea life? His over-sized flippers – otherwise known as size 17 feet.

The first official international football match was played at the West of Scotland Cricket Club in Partick in 1872, between Scotland and England.

A total of 22 players scored in the penalty shoot-out between Ivory Coast and Cameroon at the African Cup Of Nations 2005; Ivory Coast won 12-11

It was 63 Grands Prix without a British winner until August 2006. David Coulthard won in Australia in 2003, the next British winner was Jenson Button in Hungary.

Sport In Numbers

15 – the age of Peter Simple, the oldest horse to win the Grand National back in 1853. The oldest jockey was Dick Saunders who was 48 when he rode Grittar to victory in 1982.

2.3 – average goals per game at the 2006 World Cup.

40mph – speed of a dart travelling to the board.

213 – aces served by Goran Ivanisevic on his way to the 2001 Wimbledon crown.

400 million – pound value of balls used by golfers each year.

55 – seconds Michael Owen and Wayne Rooney, England's first-choice strike partnership, played together at the 2006 World Cup.

7.6 – miles surfed by Steve King to set a new world record recently.

0.25% – growth in German economy attributable to the World Cup.

2 – grey horses to win the Grand National. The Lamb won it in 1868 and 1871 and Nicholaus Silver won it in 1961.

7 – seconds it took for Freddie Eastwood to score on his Southend debut.

0 – Goals conceded by Switzerland in being knocked out of the 2006 World Cup.

The first foreigner to win England's Footballer Of The Year was Man City's German goalkeeper Bert Trautmann in 1956 – who once famously played on after breaking his neck. The next was another German, Jurgen Klinsman, almost 40 years later in 1995.

A total of 22 players scored in the penalty shoot-out between Ivory Coast and Cameroon at the African Cup Of Nations 2005, a record in international football; Ivory Coast won 12-11.

The longest match played in Wimbledon's history lasted 369 minutes, as Mark Knowles and Daniel Nestor beat Simon Aspelin and Todd Perry 5–7, 6–3, 6–7, 6–3, 23–21 in the men's doubles.

Luol Deng, the Brixton-raised Chicago Bulls basketball star – and Britain's highest-paid sportsman – is the son of a former deputy prime minister of Sudan.

Ryan Giggs was the first player to win back-to-back PFA Young Player of the Year awards in 1992 and 1993.

The lowest points total won by Premiership winners came in 1997 when Man United took the crown with just 75 points.

The smallest ever FA Cup-winning captain was Sunderland's 1973 skipper Bobby Kerr who was a diminutive 5 ft 4 ins.

An unnamed bidder paid £26,400 for the ball hit by West Indies legend Garry Sobers for six sixes in an over.

The highest break (68) in the 2006 Snooker World Championship Final, made by winner Graeme Dott, was the lowest in finals history.

£12m was paid to buy the horse "The Green Monkey" – a world-record price. The stud has not raced and is no longer in training.

Roger Federer only served five double faults in winning Wimbledon in 2006.

Recently retired Australian cricketer Justin Langer has black belts in Tai kwon do and zen do kai.

Micah Richards is only the second player with the initials MR to represent England. The first was Michael Ricketts.

Two Juventus youth team players died after trying to retrieve a ball from a lake at the club's Turin training ground.

Five Nuggets About Barcelona

1. Futbol Club Barcelona were formed in 1899 by a group of Swiss, Catalan and English men.
2. They now have 151,000 members, who effectively own the club. There are 1,782 recognised Barça fanclubs throughout the world.
3. The fans are nicknamed "Culés", which translates into "arses". It's not an insult – in the early days, the backsides of the top row of fans could be seen from outside the ground.
4. Barcelona claim to have won 106 trophies in the club's history, including 18 Spanish League titles and two European Cups. But they lost the World Club Championship Final to Independiente of Argentina.
5. Barcelona finally took a shirt sponsor in 2006, donating £1m a year to children's charity UNICEF to carry their logo. They had refused shirts sponsors previously to that.

Top Ten Pub Facts About, er, Pubs

1. Beer remains Britain's favourite alcoholic drink, accounting for 43% of pub sales.
2. Punch Taverns plc is the largest pub and bar operator in the United Kingdom, with 9,500 tenanted and managed pubs out of the total 61,000.
3. 34% of couples met or had their first date in a pub.
4. Approximately a fifth of pubs and bars shut by eleven o'clock at the latest, and roughly half by midnight.

5. US President George W. Bush fulfilled his ambition of visiting a 'genuine English pub' during his November 2003 state visit to the UK when he had lunch and a pint of non-alcoholic lager with Tony Blair at the *Dun Cow* in Sedgefield, County Durham.

6. Pubs with 'Crown' in their title are the most popular in the United Kingdom, followed by those with 'Red Lion' and 'Royal Oak'.

7. Early pubs became so commonplace that in 965, King Edgar decreed that there should be no more than one alehouse per village. In 1393, King Richard II compelled landlords to erect signs outside their premises. The legislation stated "Whosoever shall brew ale in the town with intention of selling it must hang out a sign, otherwise he shall forfeit his ale."

8. Ball's Pond Road in Islington, London was named after a pub run by Mr Ball that had a pond to the rear of the premises filled with ducks. For a small fee, drinkers could go out and take their chance at shooting the fowl.

9. Outside Ireland, Germany has more Irish pubs than any other country. In 1995, Guinness opened 85 new pubs in Germany – the same number of new McDonald's outlets.

10 JD Wetherspoon isn't a real person. The name 'Wetherspoon' was one of founder Tim Martin's teachers, who once wrote in his school report that Martin would amount to nothing. The JD part came from Uncle Jesse Duke from *The Dukes of Hazzard*, one of Martin's favourite TV shows.